D1169835

CONCILIUM

concilium 1996/3

PENTECOSTAL MOVEMENTS AS AN ECUMENICAL CHALLENGE

Edited by

Jürgen Moltmann and
Karl-Josef Kuschel

SCM Press · London
Orbis Books · Maryknoll

Published by SCM Press Ltd, 9–17 St Albans Place, London N1
and by Orbis Books, Maryknoll, NY 10545

ISBN: 0 334 03038 2 (UK)
ISBN: 1 57075 072 6 (USA)

Typeset at The Spartan Press Ltd, Lymington, Hants
Printed by Mackays of Chatham, Kent

Concilium Published February, April, June, August, October, December.

Contents

Preface

Catholic, Protestant and Orthodox theology has far too long overlooked the fact that the Pentecostal movements have become a spiritual and political force. Whereas the membership of the traditional churches is declining, that of the Pentecostal churches is rising – all over the world. From the insignificant beginnings of a Black community in Azusa Street, Los Angeles, these churches have now developed into a mass movement with more than 400 million adherents, represented also, and particularly, in great urban centres from New York through Mexico City to Seoul. By contrast, Europe has largely remained untouched by this charismatic movement.

So we have set two aims for this issue of *Concilium*, from the section on ecumenism. First, it gives information about the history of this great movement, now almost a century old, and about the internal plurality and internationalism of these Christian churches. This survey article will introduce our readers to phenomena which are indispensable for understanding the global religious situation of our time. From the origin and spread of the Pentecostal movements in particular we can see how little use our confessionalist schemes now are for grasping the complexity of the phenomena of even the Christian world.

Secondly, it engages in dialogue with representatives of the Pentecostal churches. This dialogue has two presuppositions. First, the readiness of the traditional theology of the church to perceive the Pentecostal movements as a challenge and take them seriously. It recognizes the fact that the sheer existence and growing acceptance of such churches among masses of Christians evidently reveal serious deficiencies in the established church and theologies. So we have refrained from reducing the challenge of the Pentecostal movement to seeking similar phenomena in the traditional churches and noting charismatic outbreaks there. Rather, we understand the Pentecostal churches as a challenge to all the established Christian churches to enquire self-critically into their theology, liturgy and pastoral work.

We have therefore asked Christian theologians from the Protestant, Catholic and Orthodox churches to respond self-critically and critically to five basic phenomena of the Pentecostal movement. No one could fail to see that the Pentecostal movements have put these five great themes – all too long neglected in traditional theology and extinct in encrusted institutions – back on the agenda: a new awareness of community – healings of the sick and the driving out of demons – speaking with tongues and prophecy – spontaneous prayer – baptism and the experience of the Spirit. At the same time we have also tried to introduce the experiences of the traditional churches critically into the dialogue. Dialogue with Pentecostals cannot be a one-way street. The slogan must be a reciprocal perception and correction – driven by one and the same Spirit of Jesus Christ.

But the Pentecostal churches, too, had a presupposition to contribute – and this is the second one. They have a concern for development within their own movement, argumentative discussion with theologians from the traditional churches. Theological argumentation and exegetical, systematic accounts of their own beliefs are not to be found in the earliest days of the Pentecostal movements. Their basic force was and is often something completely different: spontaneity, not academic discussion; spiritual experience, not systematic argumentation.

But today a generation of Pentecostals has grown up which need not be afraid of comparisons with the theology of the traditional churches in academic discussion or in exegetical and systematic development of the faith. The establishment of universities and seminaries, the founding of journals, and the production of theological literature from the Pentecostal movement represent nothing less than an offer of dialogue and co-operation in the conflicting fields of a Christian ecumene. Indeed, the perhaps surprising result of our dialogue volume is that there are only a few fundamental differences between the traditional churches and the new Pentecostal churches, and there are many common factors.

Because of this, the concluding article has not attempted to synthesize all the different approaches to dialogue and plural phenomena, or to evaluate the process theologically. The intention is rather to illuminate the central theme of which the Pentecostal churches have made us particularly aware and which has the same urgency for all Christian churches: a theology of the Holy Spirit as a theology of life – understood as a theology of the renewal of the people of God, all creatures, indeed the whole earth, brought about by the Spirit. If in future this governs the theology and practice of all the Christian churches, then the ecumenical challenge of the Pentecostal movements will have fulfilled its meaning.

Jürgen Moltmann
Karl-Josef Kuschel

I · Overview

From Azusa Street to the Toronto Phenomenon: Historical Roots of the Pentecostal Movement

Walter J. Hollenweger

The Pentecostal movement is the most rapidly growing missionary movement in the world. A growth of from zero to 400 million in ninety years is unprecedented in the whole of church history. There are specialists who expect that in the next century it will overshadow the Catholic Church numerically (for the statistics see VI below): every *day* 8,000 people leave the Catholic Church in Latin America. Most of them join Pentecostal churches. (This headlong growth also has its problems, as we shall see.) In Europe the growth is modest except in Catholic or Orthodox countries like France, Italy and Romania.

Despite the significance of the Pentecostal movement and the danger it poses to the established churches, academic study of it by professional theologians is almost ridiculously insignificant. In Europe, for example, there are no recognized specialists, no libraries on the topic, no competent doctorate supervisors for the many Pentecostal theologians who want to acquire academic qualifications. Most of what can be found in the academic libraries is either propaganda from the Pentecostals or apologetic from the historical churches.

This is the case although there are already some hundred dissertations by Pentecostals and many academic journals (for a bibliography see pp. 13f. below). Among Pentecostals in North America and Latin America, and also to a lesser degree in Europe, Africa and Asia, there are proven exegetes, historians and systematic theologians with a university training whom we ignore to our detriment.

What is the reason for the tremendous growth of the Pentecostal movement? The reason which the Pentecostals themselves give is the experience of the Holy Spirit. This answer is not wrong, but is inadequate, since the Holy Spirit normally works through individuals and traditions. So first, here is an account of the historical traditions.

I. The Black oral root

The most important root of the Pentecostal and charismatic movements is a revival in a Black church on Azusa Street in Los Angeles under the leadership of the Black ecumenist William J. Seymour (1870–1922: Synan). Behaviour there was sometimes very enthusiastic, sometimes also with physical phenomena like weeping, speaking with tongues, falling about, visions and so on. The journalists of the time described these 'crazy niggers' in sensational reports, since they did not know what had really happened. The members of the Azusa assembly did not deny the concomitant phenomena which were described, but they saw the nucleus of this revival in an ecumenical spirituality which transcended race and class. For the first time in the history of the USA, White church leaders (sometimes from the racist South) were ready to have hands laid on them in a community led by Blacks in order to achieve a spiritual breakthrough. And that was in 1906! The Pentecostal movement is also the only world-wide Christian church community known to me which was founded by a Black Christian – of course with the exception of Christianity itself, which was not founded by a European but by an oriental story-teller and healer.

Like earliest Christianity, the Los Angeles community was also stamped by oral culture. It had taken this over from the African legacy of the Black slaves (in the same way as jazz, spirituals and the civil rights movement under Martin Luther King). Proclamation took place not in doctrinal statements but in songs, not in theses but in dances, not in definitions but in descriptions. The first confession of faith did not even contain a definition of rebirth and baptism in the Spirit. Speaking with tongues was mentioned only peripherally (but it was a daily experience), and adult baptism was not thought worth mentioning. What held believers together was not expressed by a systematic account of faith or a creed, but by the fellowship that was experienced, by songs and prayers, by active participation in liturgy and diaconia.

From Los Angeles this revival spread all over the world. The main areas to which it spread were on the one hand certain Third World countries and on the other countries stamped by Catholic culture. In Europe and in the White Pentecostal churches of North America the Black heritage was covered over by a conservative middle-class culture. Ecumenical collaboration was fought against. Racisim displaced the original culture of reconciliation. Participatory community structures were replaced by authoritarian leading bodies. The participation of everyone in liturgy and diaconia was replaced by a professional pastorate and cleverly thought out systems of financing. Especially in the USA, many Pentecostals allied themselves with right-wing extremist groups, e.g. Pat Robertson, who played an important role in the founding of the 'Christian Coalition'. Robertson helped the Republicans to their electoral victory and was even a serious candidate for the presidency. But here, too, there are beginnings of rediscovering the roots of the movement: for example the General Secretary of the South African Council of Churches, Frank Chikane, was a Pentecostal pastor. He became involved in the fight against apartheid and was sent to prison several times as a result. Martin Luther King's 'infantry' were often members of the great Black Pentecostal 'Church of God in Christ'. Latin American Pentecostals are beginning to become interested in ecumenism and the theology of liberation (Sepúlveda).

The so-called independent churches in the Third World are a special chapter. In most cases they go back to Pentecostal missionaries, but then they became independent and developed further without missionaries. That can be seen particularly clearly among the so-called Zionists in South Africa (Hollenweger, *The Pentecostals* I, ch. 12), but also among the Aladura Churches in West Africa, the Spiritual Churches in Ghana, the Pentecostal Guru Churches in India (Hoerschelmann) and the Shamanitic Pentecostal Churches in Korea. However, scholars argue as to whether these churches should be included in the Pentecostal movement. Still, when they appear in the ecumenical context they put themselves in the Pentecostal tradition. David Barrett for good reasons includes them in the statistics relating to Pentecostals in his *World Christian Encyclopaedia*. However, it has to be realized that in no case are they to be compared with churches like the Assemblies of God, since they have developed their pre-Christian traditions on the basis of the oral communication structures taken over from the missionaries and also known to them in other ways.

II. The Catholic root

There are reasons why the Pentecostal movement has spread above all in Catholic culture, since it is not – as is commonly assumed – a typically Protestant church. It has taken over many elements from Catholicism which were mediated by John Wesley, the founder of the Methodist Church, and the American Holiness movement (Wesley translated many Catholic books for his lay preachers). These elements include:

(a) The doctrine of free will (whereas as is well known, the Reformers rejected this 'Catholic doctrine').

(b) An episcopal church structure: even where the Pentecostal leaders are not called 'bishops', they exercise episcopal authority. In fact they have 'the keys of heaven and hell' in their hands – something that many observers note critically.

(c) Reality is divided into a 'natural' and a 'supernatural' realm, as in pre-conciliar Catholicism. The laws of nature rule in the natural realm, and the supernatural laws in the supernatural realm. The latter are articulated by the 'bishops', though here of course sometimes different 'bishops' arrive at opposed statements, which are expressed in the many divisions in the church.

(d) They teach an 'order of salvation' (baptism plus baptism in the Spirit; conversion plus baptism in the Spirit; or something similar), which provides for a graded order in the appropriation of salvation. Grace is quantified. One can have 'more' grace and Spirit than the ordinary Christian – a doctrine which, as we know, was challenged by the Reformers.

So it is not surprising that for twenty years the Vatican Secretariat for Unity has been having an intensive dialogue with the Pentecostals in which both differences and agreements between the Vatican and the Pentecostals are zealously discussed (Sandidge; Bittlinger). Many Pentecostals in Latin America have argued critically but knowledgably with the Catholic theology of liberation and taken over important parts of it (Sepúlveda), while the Catholic base communities have readily learned from the 'oral culture' and musical culture of the Pentecostalists. However, sometimes one gets the impression that in the Vatican the left hand does not know what the right hand is doing. How else could one understand the polemical outbursts of the Holy Father against the Pentecostals, in which he calls them 'ravening wolves' (Cleary)?

III. The evangelical root

Occasionally Pentecostalists describe themselves as fundamentalists. However, that is to misunderstand themselves, for fundamentalism, first, is younger than the Pentecostal movement and secondly, was and is its most bitter opponent (Spittler, 'Are Pentecostals and Charismatics Fundamentalists?'). By contrast the forerunners of present-day evangelicalism were pacifists. The Pentecostals initially took over this tradition, because they recognized the connection between wars and capitalism (bibliography in Hollenweger, *Pentecostals* I, chs. 14 and 15). One can hardly imagine what will happen when the young Pentecostal historians discover their own roots, which do not at all correspond to the present-day image of the Pentecostal churches. Moreover, the first Pentecostal community was a Black, but integrated, community. It built on the tradition of the Holiness preachers, who were the first to help the Black slaves to escape from their masters. They founded universities at which Black people and women were trained, something that the church establishment of the time could only describe as immoral and revolutionary. They also dedicated themselves to a peace plan similar to the present-day United Nations Organization – all things which have been and are rejected by the fundamentalists. Moreover, the Pentecostal movement is neither theologically nor ethically monolithic. In this respect it is even more pluralistic than Catholicism. For example, today there are both Pentecostal pacifists and Pentecostal military chaplains. There are churches which baptize infants and churches which baptize adults (Robeck).

There is even a broad spectrum of opinion in matters of sexual ethics, the definition of baptism in the Spirit, social and individual ethics, the question of biblical hermeneutics, the doctrine of the Trinity and christology. Therefore talk of 'the doctrine' of the Pentecostal churches is highly problematical. What unites the Pentecostal churches is not a doctrine but a religious experience, and this can be interpreted and substantiated in very different ways. Part of the reason for its variety is that the Pentecostalists took over many rites and views from their pre-Christian cultures and recognized them as gifts of the Holy Spirit. Moreover, the first Pentecostal pioneers came from a variety of churches (including the Catholic Church) and brought theological and liturgical traditions with them from their pre-Pentecostal existence.

IV. The critical root

Right from the beginning, the Pentecostal movement has developed a critical theology and social ethics, though today this is being submerged in the din of Pentecostal propaganda, despite the fact that many Pentecostal exegetes with a university training are working in accordance with the generally recognized rules of historical-critical research. However, as in other churches, these insights have hardly penetrated the communities, just as most members of the Pentecostal churches have hardly any inkling of the ecumenical commitment of many of their leaders.

Not a few of the young Pentecostal theologians are joining in the fight for justice, and they also occasionally criticize practices of the Catholic Church which do not conform with liberation theology. Right from the start, Pentecostalist missiologists criticized mission which understood itself as a transfer of European and American ideology. They supported and therefore encouraged the formation of indigenous churches. Today, however, they are confronted with a pluralism in their former mission churches before which they are helpless both theologically and in terms of mission policy.

A critical attitude has also developed in ecclesiology, pneumatology and ethics at the level of theological reflection. For example, I found the most well-reasoned criticism of the Toronto Blessing and the American television and healing evangelists in the Pentecostal learned journals. The Pentecostals have already burned their fingers several times. They know the devastating consequences that a confusion of the 'American Way of Life' (or even a petty-bourgeois individualistic ethic) has for Christianity. They have experienced this in their own body. It is all the more regrettable that professional theologians, Catholic and Protestant, neither know nor support these critical Pentecostal theologians. To mention some of the most important of them: the Croatian Pentecostalist Miroslav Volf gained his doctorate with Jürgen Moltmann for a brilliant dissertation on 'work' in which he skilfully grappled with Marx and the Western understanding of work. He is now teaching in the theological college in Osijek and at Fuller Theological Seminary in Pasadena, California. The same could be said of Peter Kuzmic, who in his dissertation at the University of Zagreb investigated the Serbo-Croat translation of the Bible. Russ Spittler, pastor of the American Assemblies of God and Professor of New Testament at Fuller Theological Seminary, among other things wrote a highly significant article on speaking with tongues, in which he demonstrated that glossolalia is a natural gift. Cecil M. Robeck, similarly a pastor of the American Assemblies of God and Professor of Ecumenics at Fuller Theological Seminary, is unswervingly committed to ecumenical collaboration and work against racism by emphasizing Seymour's significance for ecumenism and church history and taking an active part in numerous dialogues arranged by the World Council of Churches and the Catholic Church. Murray W. Dempster, who is also a pastor of the American Assemblies of God, editor of *Pneuma* and a theological teacher in San Francisco, has written important works on social ethics. The van Laan brothers in Holland are grappling profoundly with the ecumenical heritage of the Dutch Pentecostal movement (there is a detailed discussion in Hollenweger, *The Pentecostals*, II).

As for the Toronto Blessing, which has already been mentioned, the Pentecostal theologians have no intrinsic objections to physical manifestations in worship. These phenomena are known from all revival movements, including revivals in the Pentecostal movement. However, in themselves they are not a sign of the Holy Spirit, but universally known religious phenomena. They only take on a spiritual quality when – as with the Pentecostal theologians who refer back to the revival in Los Angeles – they are put at the service of peace, when their power is shown in the overcoming of barriers of race and class, of poverty, oppression and meaninglessness.

V. The ecumenical root

All the Pentecostal churches began as an ecumenical revival movement. This movement did not want to found new churches, but to bring life to existing ones. In some places it succeeded in remaining ecumenical. But for the most part it developed into separate denominations. As an example of early ecumenical commitment I might mention the founder of the German Pentecostal movement, Jonathan Paul (1853–1931), who until his death remained a Lutheran pastor and baptized children. The founder of the English Pentecostal movement was Alexander A. Boddy (1854–1930), an Anglican priest to the end of his life. In France it was the Reformed pastor Louis Dallière (1897–1976), who at a very early stage sought contact with Jews, Orthodox and Catholics. I have already mentioned the basic ecumenical attitude of William J. Seymour. From more recent times, reference might be made to David Du Plessis (1905–1987). He came originally from South Africa but later lived in California and worked indefatigably for the ecumenical involvement of Pentecostals. The co-president of the Vatican-Pentecostal dialogue is Cecil M. Robeck, mentioned above, who is working untiringly for ecumenical concerns with his Catholic co-president, the Benedictine Kilian McDonnell. Today, twelve Pentecostal churches are members of the World Council of Churches. Some of these are major churches. In England most Black Pentecostal churches are members of the British Council of Churches, and some are members of the Conference of European Churches. So the first Pentecostal member churches of the Conference of European Churches are Black. This is also significant (Gerloff). In Latin America, many Pentecostal churches are involved in the Consejo Latinamericano de Iglesias, at whose conferences they are an important factor.

There are countries in which the ecumenical movement is exclusively or mainly represented by the Pentecostal churches, since otherwise it has no member churches worth mentioning (e.g. in Chile or in Congo-

Brazzaville). In North America a number of Pentecostal theologians are collaborating with 'Faith and Order'.

However, most of the Pentecostal church authorities are (still) opposed to or at least reserved about the ecumenical movement. This is the case, although already at the 1968 General Assembly of the World Council of Churches in Uppsala a Pentecostal leader from Germany gave a report in the plenary session about the relationship between the ecumenical movement and the Pentecostal movement.

How is it possible for an originally ecumenical movement to have developed in this way? The ecumenical scheme for development can be sketched out as follows:

Phase 1: An ecumenical revival movement which wants to serve all churches.

Phase 2: The foundation of local communities, the building of churches.

Phase 3: National and international alliances, the production of catechisms and confessions of faith, the establishment of Bible schools and theological colleges, pension funds for pastors, etc.

Phase 4: New reflection on the ecumenical roots, acceptance of dialogue with the Vatican and the World Council of Churches.

Each phase lasts around twenty-five years, a generation. The so-called classical Pentecostal churches (like the Assemblies of God or the Church of God (Cleveland)) are now between the third and fourth stages, whereas the so-called charismatic renewal in the historical churches can be put between the first and second phases. Granted, it is still claimed that the Pentecostal movements are a movement within the church, but the trend towards the foundation of independent communities can be traced clearly (usually under terms like 'building up the community' or 'church growth'). Here the Catholic churches can deal better with this revival within the church than the Protestant churches.

VI. Historiography, statistics, bibliography

Until recently there was no agreement in the Pentecostal movement over the roots of their own church. Some derived it almost exclusively from the American Holiness Movement, with the American racist Charles Fox Parham (1873–1929) as its connecting link. It was in his Bible school that William J. Seymour was able to follow what Parham said about the Holy Spirit behind the half-opened doors. Others see the origin of their church in William J. Seymour's revival in Los Angeles. These different historical assessments contain a theological evaluation. If the Pentecostal movement is characterized above all by the experience of baptism in the Spirit (with speaking in tongues), then its founder is Charles Fox Parham. But if the working of the Holy Spirit is understood not only in religious crisis experiences but equally in the power of the Spirit which both reconciles and is critical of the spirit of the age, then its founder is William J. Seymour. The Assemblies of God (USA) and many Third World Pentecostals have decided for the second definition.

At present there is no global history of the Pentecostal movement. In my own handbook of the Pentecostal movement (available only in German, see the bibliography), I described the Pentecostal churches in all countries of the earth with important source-texts in the original languages. This handbook is now out of date but has not been replaced. In a sense the *Dictionary of Pentecostal and Charismatic Movements* has taken up the continuation of the handbook. However, it concentrates on North America with some important excursuses on the European Pentecostal movement. The important Third World churches do not appear in it. The value of this reference work consists in the fact that the authors come from all the Pentecostal *and* non-Pentecostal traditions of North America (including the Catholic tradition). Here the Catholic religious Peter Hocken is particularly important. The bibliographies (Jones), too, cover only the American scene. By contrast, the Pentecostal professional journals mentioned in the bibliography provide up-to-date information about the development world-wide. A discussion of the literature country by country would go beyond the bounds of this article.

VII. National and international associations

In some countries and regions the various Pentecostal denominations have united in umbrella organizations, like the British Pentecostal Fellowship. The Pentecostal Fellowship of North America, to which only White Pentecostal churches were admitted, was dissolved in 1994. A new body, the 'Pentecostal/Charismatic Churches of North America', was founded, in which the Black churches have equal rights. With explicit reference to the founder, William J. Seymour, the racial war between Black and White Pentecostals was settled. The Whites openly confessed 'their participation in the sin of racism by their silence, their rejection and their blindness'.

In Europe there is the Pentecostal European Conference and in loose association with it the European Pentecostal Theological Association (EPTA), which regularly holds scholarly theological conferences. The Society for Pentecostal Studies in North America has the same function.

The conference reports of these two academic associations are good indications of what is coming up in the Pentecostal movement (obtainable from the *EPTA Bulletin* or *Pneuma*).

The World Pentecostal Conferences (the first was held in Zurich in 1947) were an international forum which discussed disputed problems within the Pentecostal churches (baptism in the Spirit, healing through prayer, questions of international collaboration). Today they have lost this character and have become a PR event dominated by the Western Pentecostal churches, without any legal or even pastoral significance. People from the Pentecostal movement who were concerned for justice and opposed to apartheid and racism never got a platform at this conference. So today it represents at most 60 million out of the 400 million Pentecostals.

VIII. The ecumenical significance

The ecumenical significance of the Pentecostal movement consists in the following points:

First, in many countries it is a church *of* the poor (not just 'a church *for* the poor', which is what Pentecostals accuse the Catholic church of being). The poor take liturgy, theology and politics into their own hands and are not – at least in the best examples – dependent on the transfer of theology and ideology from the power centres of the West.

Secondly, it is a church which can no longer be grasped with our confessional theological categories. But that could already have been noted from a study of the historical confessions. There is more in common between certain evangelical and certain Catholic Christians than within their relevant confessions. The confessional families no longer correspond to present practices of distinction and grouping. That has far-reaching consequences for the ecumenical debate which – whether Catholic or Protestant – still regards theological ideas as being also normative for confessional identification.

Thirdly, the Pentecostal movement is a decided theological and social factor in the Third World, because it gives people a face, dignity and independence. That also has consequences for politics, of the kind that one can pursue, for example, in South Africa.

Fourthly, the Pentecostal movement confronts us with the basic question of what theology really is. Is theology only what is taught in our universities, i.e. a rational systematic discourse based on Aristotelian logic, which operates with concepts and definitions? Or could it not be that for example the parables of Jesus, the stories of the Old Testament, the hymns of the Reformation, the stories of the saints in the Catholic and Orthodox traditions, are also theology, but in other categories? If the latter is the case, then what does this mean for theology as a university discipline and for ecumenical community?

Translated by John Bowden

A Select Bibliography

Abbreviations

IC   Studien zur interkulturellen Geschichte des Christentums, Frankfurt, Bern, Paris and New York.
Dictionary   Stanley M. Burgess et al. (ed.), *Dictionary of Pentecostal and Charismatic Movements*, Grand Rapids, Mich. 1988.

D. B. Barrett, *World Christian Encyclopedia*, Nairobi 1982.
–, 'Statistics, Global', *Dictionary*, 810–29.
A. Bittlinger, *Papst und Pfingstler. Der römisch-katholischer/pfingstlicher Dialog und seine ökumenische Relevanz*, IC 16, 1978.
– (ed.), *The Church is Charismatic. The World Council of Churches and the Charismatic Renewal*, Geneva 1981.
F. Chikane, *No Life of My Own*, Maryknoll 1988.
E. Cleary, 'John Paul Cries "Wolf"; Misreading the Pentecostals', *Commonweal* 199, 20 November 1992, 7f.
M. W. Dempster, 'Pentecostal Social Concern and the Biblical Mandate of Social Justice', *Pneuma* 9/2, Autumn 1987, 129–53.
R. Gerloff, *A Plea for British Black Theologies. The Black Church Movement in Britain and its Transatlantic Cultural and Theological Interaction*, IC 77, 1992 (2 vols.).
P. Hocken, 'European Pentecostalism', *Dictionary*, 268–78.
W. Hoerschelmann, *Christliche Gurus. Darstellung von Selbstverständnis und Funktion indigenen Christseins durch unabhängige, charismatisch geführte Gruppen in Sudindien*, IC 12, 1977.
W. J. Hollenweger, *Handbuch der Pfingstbewegung*, 1966–68 (10 vols.), available from Yale Divinity School, New Haven, Conn.
–, *The Pentecostals*, I, Peabody, Mass. 1988.
–, *The Pentecostals* II, Peabody, Mass 1996.
C. E. Jones, *A guide to the Study of Pentecostal Movements* (2 vols.), ATLA Bibliography Series no. 6, Metuchen, NJ 1979.
C. van der Laan, *Sectarian Against His Will: Gerrit Roelof Polman and the Birth of Pentecostalism in the Netherlands*, Studies in Evangelicalism 11, Metuchen, NJ and London 1991.
C. M. Robeck, 'The Ecclesiology of Koinonia and Baptism', *Journal of Ecumenical Studies*, 27/3, Summer 1990, 504–34.
J. L. Sandidge, *Roman Catholic/Pentecostal Dialogue (1977–1982). A Study in Developing Ecumenism*, IC 44, 1987 (2 vols.).
J. Sepúlveda, 'Pentecostalism and Liberation Theology: Two Manifestations of the Work of the Holy Spirit for the Renewal of the Church', in H. D. Hunter and

P. Hocken (eds.), *All Together in One Place. Theological Papers from the Brighton Conference on World Evangelization*, Sheffield 1993, 51–63.

R. Spittler, 'Glossolalia', *Dictionary*, 250–4.

–, 'Are Pentecostals and Charismatics Fundamentalists? A Review of American Uses of these Categories', in Karla Poewe (ed.), *Charismatic Christianity as a Global Culture*, Columbia 1994, 103–16.

M. Volf, 'Materiality of Salvation: An Investigation in the Soteriologies of Liberation and Pentecostal Theologies', *Journal of Ecumenical Studies* 26/3, Spring 1989, 447–67.

Journals

EPTA Bulletin, The Journal of the European Pentecostal Theological Association (Elim Bible College, London Road, Nantwich CW5 6LW, England).

Pneuma. The Journal of the Society for Pentecostal Studies (PO Box 2671, Gaithersburg, MD 20886, USA).

Journal of Pentecostal Theology (Sheffield Academic Press, 19 Kingfield Rd, Sheffield S11 9AS, England).

II · Dialogues

We are the Church: New Congregationalism

A Pentecostal Perspective

Harold D. Hunter

Readers familiar with *Concilium* might take the title of this article to imply a particular ecclesiastical polity. This is not true for Pentecostals, who bring to life the admission in the Lima document *Baptism, Eucharist and Ministry*[1] that the 'New Testament does not describe a single pattern of ministry which might serve as a blueprint or continuing norm for all future ministry in the Church'. This view of the essence of the church differs from that of those who insist that we really cannot talk about the nature of the church without making certain fundamental assumptions about how the church is to be constituted. Is it an episcopate, with a council of presbyters, or simply a congregation? The Assemblies of God officially use the word 'fellowship' as their corporate self-designation because they resist accepting their status as a denomination.

I. The third force in Christianity

In contrast to what is sometimes advertised as the monolithic character of Pentecostalism, it is the considerable diversity that complicates the process of clearly identifying what is 'Pentecostal'. The ubiquity of the international Pentecostal-charismatic movement as it launches into the twenty-first century outdistances attempts at classification and clarification. In the face of descriptions such as patchwork quilt, rainbow, kaleidoscope, mosaic and umbrella, it may be appropriate to apply to Pentecostalism Dom Gregory Dix's verdict on the Church of England, for global Pentecostalism is truly an 'amorphous mass of Pelagian good will'.

The designation by Bishop Lesslie Newbigin and Henry P. Van Dusen of classical Pentecostalism as the third force in twentieth-century Christianity reflects Newbigin's paradigm of order, faith and experience. The following is an exploratory paradigm that seeks to move towards identifying streams of Christianity that will continue into the next millennium.

Apostolic

Succession	*Teaching*	*Restoration*
Catholic	Magisterial Reformation:	Pentecostals
Orthodox	Lutheran	Believers' churches:
Anglican	Presbyterian	Baptists
		Wesleyanism

Pentecostals would answer with a hearty 'Amen!' when *Baptism, Eucharist and Ministry* emphasizes that the community lives 'in the power of the Spirit . . . characterized by a variety of charisms'. The ability of *Baptism, Eucharist and Ministry* to arrive at several important convergences should encourage Pentecostalists from all over the world to sense a welcome opportunity to participate in the future of the conciliar movement. Although they are distracted by the absence of their doctrinal and pastoral priorities, their greatest loss may be the lack of redress by *Baptism, Eucharist and Ministry* to anything like the Pentecostal ethos. Since Pentecostal praxis anticipated Bonhoeffer's concept of 'cheap grace', this is not a minor oversight.

Tensions between the institutional and the charismatic have appeared throughout canonical and ecclesiastical history. Although the Pentecostal movement is an obvious testimony to the belief in releasing charisms in the community of the faithful, in reality many gifts have been suppressed by dominating authority figures and structures. Most Pentecostals seem to deny the continuance of special revelation unique to scripture, while owning contemporary charismatic insights and inspirations. This in turn has given rise to bureaucracies and shibboleth monitors rivalling the older Roman Catholic magisterium. The theological problem may differ little from that raised by the existence of the 'inerrant' Roman Catholic teaching office. Pentecostals must rise above this internal struggle and reckon with the description of the World Council of Churches by the first General Secretary as 'essentially an attempt to manifest the economy of the charismata'.

II. The local church at the centre

Yet one common feature distinguishes Pentecostal churches. Even with the most rigid control from the top down, the local churches are constantly exhorted to be alive and on fire. Each member is expected to be active and carry the flame. To bend a familiar image, Pentecostals believe in the transubstantiation not of elements or buildings, but of believers. It is in the context of determining the nature of worship – though in a forum sometimes labelled the 'sacred theatre of the spirit possessed' – that Pentecostals go on to the question of the church dispersed in the world – that is, the witnessing and serving people of God.

Since Pentecostals do not seek a radical departure from their inherited theology but rather its vivification, the term 'experience', which is denigrated in the West, fails to capture the intended personal appropria-tion of biblical truths. If their narrative theology has at times been uneasy with mainstream formulations of gospel truth, the same cannot be said about the Pentecostal resolve to adhere to perceived fundamentals of the faith.

Many of the Pentecostal movement's pioneers in the USA exerted considerable energy in removing what they saw as the debris of skilfully worded yet irrelevant, if not damaging, creeds which had led most of Christendom astray. However, when current Pentecostal leaders examine documents like the Apostles' Creed, they often find themselves unable to fault the contents. They unconsciously give credit to the description of the Nicene-Constantinopolitan Creed as providing the church 'East and West, Catholic and Evangelical alike, with its one authentically ecumenical confession of faith'.

Although the Faith and Order Commission of the World Council of Churches has made considerable progress toward the elimination of various societal barriers, it remains possible that *Baptism, Eucharist and Ministry* encompasses remnants of an unintentional socio-economic bias. The Pentecostal movement represents different layers of socio-economic strata from those of the creators of *Baptist, Eucharist and Ministry*. The paucity of scholars available to respond to *Baptism, Eucharist and Ministry* is something of an acquiescence in the socio-economic realities familiar to non-whites in the Third World.

III. Oral narrative and praxis

The Pentecostal movement's universal predilection for oral narrative and praxis is not incidentally related to the belief that pneumatic experience subject to extensive analysis can become entombed in layers of theological formulas which do not stimulate the faithful. A not-distant echo of the crux of the matter is found in speculation about whether Emil Brunner's *The Divine-Human Encounter* had any bearing on the interest in Pentecostals displayed by the likes of Dr Eduard Schweizer. Interestingly, Emil Brunner was not only Professor of Dogmatics at the University of Zurich, but he held professorial rank in the department of preaching. Consider the constant Pentecostal preoccupation with seeking 'the anointing' when preaching.

Studies in the Hebrew canon which have emphasized the power of the spoken word are relevant. For the Pentecostal masses it is evident that the spoken word effects action. Writing about the oral dimension of popular Roman Catholic Hispanic religiosity, Sixto T. García notes that Heidegger and Gadamer reminded us that poets give life to the specific form of being that their verses bear within themselves. Gerhard Lohfink says that the reason for the use of narrative is not the assumption that simple people are incapable of thinking in abstract ways, but the fact that narrative 'presentifies'.

Pentecostals can argue that since we are given our reality to begin with as individuals, when we are restored as lost and alienated to the fellowship of God our Maker, our salvation does not consist in being absorbed into some philosophic absolute; rather we are saved as individuals. This is the truth of Kierkegaard's emphasis against Hegel when he talked about 'that individual' and said that on his tombstone the only epitaph he desired was 'that individual'.

This question, perhaps, had something to do with Emil Brunner's problem with the distinction between the visible and invisible church. He complained that it is one of the scandals of Christendom that in Christian nations the visible church is so inclusive as to include the great majority in the population; but the actual practising or confessing church is a very minuscule minority within this larger, all-inclusive, nominal Christian church. Everyone in Denmark, as Kierkegaard complained, is Evangelical Lutheran. In his *Attack on Christendom*, Kierkegaard complained of this bitterly, saying that we try to fool God, muddle him with all the millions of name Christians that we have in Denmark, so that he will not perceive that in reality there is not one true Christian in all of Denmark.

The explosion in mainstream academia of investigations into various facets of the oral dimension of early Christianity is instructive. The axiomatic antithesis between reflective theology and expressive narrative has been successfully challenged. Meanwhile, it is ironic to see scholars 'rediscover' the 'narrative innocence' of pre-Hellenistic Christianity while spurning historical and contemporary manifestations of the same phenomenon.

There is irony in the scholarly disdain heaped on the myths that are part of the fabric of Pentecostalism. Many of these same scholars highly esteem sections of canonical materials which they judge to be mythical. The inconsistency of valuing one set of myths while unilaterally condemning all such things when they are associated with Pentecostalism may demonstrate an ethnocentric view of reality.

Analysis of the belief-systems of ordinary people has often been held in disrepute by intellectuals and always provided an easy target. The lack of interest in popular religiosity can be measured by the level of disinterest among theologians towards teachings prevalent among their own enclaves. Voices from the pew have been muffled or conveniently not heard. Theological tomes, erudite expositions and conciliar documents virtually eliminate any concern for interacting with grass-roots thinking.

The academy and magisterial Christianity have had their suspicions of popular Christianity confirmed as Pentecostalism has celebrated its African roots and given prominence to women and those without formal education. Yet Pentecostal ecclesiarchs should have some fears allayed by the healthy respect for Scripture evident in *Baptism, Eucharist and Ministry* and the absence of a sense of an arid academic enterprise of disaffected intellectuals. *Confessing The One Faith*'s depiction of Nicene thought as 'doxological' and 'confessional' fits well in categorizing Pentecostals over against the 'historical-critical' preoccupation of modernity.

Enrique Dussel argues that the 1492 discovery of Amerindia moved Europe from being a periphery of the East to the centre of the Atlantic Ocean and the Mediterranean Sea. Dussel's 'trans-modernity' finds the Other not only diachronically, but also synchronically. Tensions between Pentecostalism and modernity have given rise to labels such as 'pre-critical' and 'sub-modern'. With the advent of postmodernity, we can celebrate this as an accomplishment, not an embarrassment. However, Pentecostalism and the charismatic movement have unwittingly been radically influenced by Gutenberg's invention (1440), making possible the world-wide parade of Bibles, along with the proliferation of defiant commentators, spawned, in part, by Luther's idea of direct access to God. A certifiable ecclesiology, on the other hand, must cope with the remarkable summation captured in the original Nicene-Constantinopolitan Creed when it gives the marks of the church as 'one, holy, catholic, and apostolic'.

Notes

1. *Baptism, Eucharist and Ministry*, Faith and Order Paper No. 111, Geneva 1982.

A Catholic Response – Base Church Communities in Brazil

Faustino Teixeira

The formation of base church communities has perhaps been the most significant and original contribution made by the church in Latin America to the universal church. When, at the end of the Synod on Evangelization in the Modern World (1974), Pope Paul VI referred to the base church communities as a hope for the whole church, he was certainly convinced of the value of their example for evangelization as a whole. At the time, the base church communities were going through their phase of creative growth. Following the lines laid down by the church renewal started at the Second Vatican Council and given a renewed impulse by the Medellín Conference (1968), base church communities became established as a 'new way of being church', characterized, above all, by their courageous option for the poor and for integral liberation.

In recent years the experience of the communities has again become a subject of discussion. Especially since the latter half of the 1980s, the base church communities in Brazil have faced a complex situation in both political and ecclesial fields. The existence of a new political situation, one of transition or 'opening-out', encourages the emergence of new channels of political presence and participation in civil society. While before, given the state of repression, the base church communities had become an outstanding focus of critical presence, the new situation is forcing them to rethink their specific identity. The international ecclesiastical situation has also shifted. The affirmation of a new Catholic identity during the pontificate of John Paul II, starting in 1978, shows the need for a 'new church balance'. Within the dynamic of the new evangelization decreed, the base church communities have ceased to occupy the outstanding place they had after the Council. In some cases, the whole liberative pastoral policy current in Latin America has been questioned, viewed with scepticism, not to say suspicion, and even persecuted.

Equally, there is no denying the influence of the collapse of 'real' socialism on the base church communities, particularly on their concept of a new society. This situation, however, has not meant a decisive end to the experiment, as many are now saying it will, since the desire for a different, life-affirming society has remained alive in the communities. The collapse of socialism has, in fact, left an enormous vacuum, and for many people has ushered in a period of great uncertainty. In the communities, though, it has implied a reworking of the experiment under a new umbrella of utopic thinking, independent of any label given it, in which commitment to the cause of life, involving building an alternative society of freedom and equality, is still their main platform. The new factor is that of taking up the struggle once more within a new overall situation, in which the emergent challenges are faced in the same way as the old ones.

A recent survey of base church communities in Brazil, covering 2965 parishes spread throughout the country, has for the first time established a reliable data base which can produce a better understanding of their current status. This survey has produced some important facts. 1. The national dimension of the phenomenon: base church communities are present in all regions of the Brazilian Bishops' National Conference. 2. Lay people play the leading role in this new way of being church: in seventy per cent of the communities established, they are responsible for the Sunday liturgy when there is no eucharistic celebration. The participation of lay people is also evident in community councils and coordination teams, which are a feature of seventy-five per cent of the communities, indicating the preponderance of a community rather than individual exercise of pastoral care. Lay people take on their pastoral responsibilities with great energy, carrying out new forms of ministry and creating new ecclesiological values. 3. The presence and power of the word of God in the communities: the survey showed that seventy-five per cent of the communities had a Bible study group, which fact in itself constitutes a significant catechetical dimension. 4. The linking of faith to social change: the survey showed that those communities that were most active in the field of pastoral action were those that also celebrated the Sunday liturgy, included Bible study groups, and were led by a community council or co-ordinating team.[1] On the basis of the information provided by the survey, the number of base church communities now in existence in Brazil and working along the renewal lines laid down by Vatican II and Medellín would be between sixty and eighty thousand.[2]

I. Base church communities: a church in the service of the kingdom

1. A church reborn from the poor through the power of the Spirit

Works produced on the base church communities show them as presenting a living image of a new way of being church, reborn from the poor under the dynamizing power of the Spirit. This new ecclesial image came about in response to the need to rediscover the church and re-make it from the bottom up. This is a real 'ecclesiogenesis', providing a motor for the radical conversion of the church to the world of the people, and showing the need for a deep renewal of church structures. With the base church communities, the church has found the possibility of recovering its rootedness in the people: a church that becomes people and a people that becomes church, in perfect reciprocity.

The community essay has led to a questioning of the usual understanding of the church, both in its relation to society and in its internal structuring. In the pastoral field, the church feels impelled to a commitment different from the one to which it was, by and large, traditionally accustomed. It has become imperative for it to adopt prophetic positions consonant with its option for the poor, and this implies breaking old alliances and establishing new ties of solidarity. On the internal level, the church also feels called to revise its operational structures, so as to enable all to take a greater share in being and building the church.

The base church communities belong to the dynamic of service of the kingdom and following of Jesus. They have a conviction, rooted in experience, that only on the basis of fidelity to the way of the Jesus of history can the church carry out its true evangelizing role. The kingdom of God, as the horizon to which this fidelity points, occupies a central place in the base church community experience, being seen as at one and the same time a free gift and a demanding call to affirmation of life. The following of Jesus and the centrality of the kingdom are indissolubly bound together in the communities. While on the one hand it is correct to state that the meaning of the kingdom cannot be understood if it is separated from Jesus, since it takes on its specific features in Jesus, on the other hand it is equally important to stress that there can be no true understanding of Jesus outside his relationship to the kingdom. The base church communities help us to understand that we cannot really concentrate on Jesus as mediator while relegating to second place the demands of bringing about the kingdom, of putting its values into practice, of seeing its implication for history as the embodiment of the Father's will. It is Jesus himself who through his consistent affirmation of life calls us all continually to be disciples of the kingdom in history.

The communities help to enrich our understanding of the church, underlining the dynamic of the following of Jesus as an essential ingredient in its essence, as well as the vivifying presence of the Spirit, which reveals its dimension of happening, of church in movement, in which values of participatory community, of faith, hope and love, can come to the fore. The community and the church dynamic of the base church communities shows the kingdom of God as the wider horizon of the church, and that the church, as the sign and instrument of the kingdom, must give continuity to Jesus' cause, to his dream of solidarity and justice in history.

2. Affirmation of the social and ecclesial citizenship of the poor

The Brazilian base church communities went through their formative process at a particularly difficult period of the country's history, characterized by intense repression of all forms of critical and popular resistance. Especially after 1968, the channels of popular organization were violently disrupted, its leadership persecuted, imprisoned, tortured or forced into exile. In this dark social and political panorama, which contrasted with the post-conciliar spring, the small communities began to emerge, one by one, re-creating forms of popular resistance on the peripheries of the cities and out in the country, re-forging bonds of solidarity and rebuilding the hope of the poor.

When freedom of expression was being most strongly repressed, the base church communities enabled the poor to affirm their citizenship as social and ecclesial subjects. Through their special organizational dynamic, these small communities opened up a space in which words could be heard or, better still, expressed. This was a remarkable initiative in breaking people's forced isolation and forging conditions in which a new citizenship became possible. Experience of community made it possible for the poor to realize their dignity and value as social agents. They experienced this as a personal enrichment, as an 'intensification of their quality as agents'.[3] In this new space, the poor were able not only to meet and express themselves, but also to feel recognized, to regain consciousness of their value, of their dignity and of their rights. The experience of 'being people', much related in innumerable accounts, is one of the essential features of the inner dynamic of the communities, picked up in their songs: 'Our vision suddenly cleared, we found the poor had worth.'

Together with this affirmation of their dignity, the poor in the base church communities were discovering the importance of the community dimension. Communities emerged as a space in which the human and social fabric could be rewoven, thereby breaking with the dominant 'dissociative' emphasis of the time. The experience of community generated a climate of sharing, affectivity, mutual recognition, exchange, sociability and solidarity. Such a climate conferred identity on the group and was the basic constituent of the emergence of a critical consciousness. The poor in community discovered that the problems afflicting them were common; they shared the discovery of their value as subjects, and acquired a critical understanding of their rights. The expressed perception of this experience of their sacred dignity as persons, with the awakening of a communal appreciation of their collective wants, was what made possible the development of effective action in the direction of social change. The poor 'taking the word' in the communities happened as a growing will to share not only in the life of the church, but also in movements seeking to change the face of society: neighbourhood associations, unions, political parties and other popular movements. And, to the extent that the communities deepened the level of their participation in social struggles, they themselves became conflictive elements within the system.

In the whole of this dynamic process of building up the citizenship of the poor within the base church communities, a basic element was their permanent reference to the word of God. It was in the process of revealing the word that the person was revealed in the communities. The word of God became the basic dimension in the shaping of the overall motivation of the poor: it was the light that illumined their situation and their source of encouragement in all their struggles. It was what brought the poor together in community, what gave the poor dignity, authority, tenacity and hope, their starting point on all journeys as a community. 'The people of God feels that political action is illuminated, strengthened and deepened by the word of God. The Bible, read in community and in the light of our situation, helps us to discover the main lines of God's plan. The word of God is the motive power for political action.'⁴

3. A participatory and wholly ministerial church

The participation of lay people is, we have seen, one of the distinguishing features of the new way of being church that has emerged from the base church communities. We are indeed witnessing a great broadening of the potentialities of lay people within the communities, as well as a notable blossoming of new ministries or services. This lay participation and these new ministries were both recognized by the Brazilian Bishops' National Conference, in a document that is still very relevant, as 'two fruits of the greatest significance for the life of the Church'.⁵ The dynamic presence of lay people can be found at all levels of the church life that throbs in the communities: interpreting the word of God, catechesis, prayers and the planning of services, sacramental and ministerial duties, community organization and evangelizing.

This emergence of lay people as bearers of an evangelizing potential implies a reworking of the ecclesial structure on more egalitarian lines. This does not remove the basic nature of church communion, since the base church communities in Brazil are deeply bound to their pastors; it does, though, bring new demands for reciprocal communion and co-responsibility in the church.

In the experience of the base church communities, the concept of the church as people of God has taken on a practical historical-social embodiment, ceasing to be simply a theoretical or metaphorical concept and taking shape in the activity of the church. Lay people in the communities really become conscious of being members of the people of God, with full ecclesial citizenship and appreciation of their rights in the church. In the innumerable accounts of the communities prepared for the inter-church meetings of base church communities which have been held in Brazil since 1975, this situation is illustrated most clearly: 'The church was four stone walls; now it's the people, persons.' 'Until I was seventy, I thought the church was a place where you prayed, but now I know we're the church.' 'We are the church of today, a living church, the whole people.' 'The church is the people understanding what God wants.'[6]

In this way, lay people feel stimulated by the dynamic of their own community to play a greater role in the church, through a more active commitment to its missionary and apostolic task. This is reflected in the vitality of new ministries, seen especially in four areas: proclamation of the gospel, celebrations of faith, planning, and action in the secular sphere. The services that are emerging are different, but all go to make up, and are seen as, a demonstration of the power and expression of the Spirit acting through its people.

The dimension of co-responsibility has become a real novelty in the way ministries are exercised in the base church communities. The collegiate form predominates both in selecting ministers and in the way they act. This more synodal approach had brought with it a powerful questioning of the more rigid and traditional parish structure, which in turn opens up new horizons for the life of the church.

In the base church communities, the fact that all take part has become a basic ecclesiological principle, and this demand to participate is not restricted to the day-to-day activities of the communities, but is broadened out into a greater presence of the communities themselves in the basic decision-making processes at diocesan level. This aspect, being more recent, has implied that there has had to be a great effort to change attitudes, since even in the more open and progressive dioceses, the decision-making process has always been very much reserved to the bishop and clergy. Significant facts have emerged from a recent pastoral analysis, showing that when the communities are kept at a distance from the diocese, their participatory character is diminished. While decisions are clearly taken on a participatory basis within the communities themselves, this becomes less clear as one moves up to more central bodies such as the parish and the diocese.[7]

It is important to stress that the emergence of new ministries within the base church communities does not happen through extinguishing or diminishing the role of traditional ministries. What happens is that they are redefined in the light of the dynamic of commitment and conversion to the impoverished. A new style of ministerial practice comes into being, characterized by co-participation, communion and closer contact with the life of the poor. Pastors rediscover their place in the communities as animators of faith, knowing how to listen, to commune, to share. The communities have helped innumerable pastors, in their work of pastoral involvement, to recover their identity as promoters and defenders of the poor.[8]

The question of new ministries has undergone extensive examination within the base church communities, with particular stress being laid on it in recent years. Even in the current context of a more suspicious official church attitude to the subject of late, the challenges are being recognized and worked through with all seriousness: the question of the permanence of non-ordained ministries; that of the need for greater sensitivity in accepting existing charisms, and of greater recognition of the right of women to share in ministerial tasks and decision-making processes; acceptance of the capacity and dignity of lay people in their exercise of ministerial roles, without relegating them to a merely 'supply' position, but even broadening their sharing in sacramental ministries.[9]

4. The base church communities in the project-process of a church of the poor

The ecclesiological standing of the base church communities has been a recurrent theme in recent reflection on them. At the sixth inter-church meeting of base church communities held in July 1986 in the city of Trindade (Goiás), this became the focus of intense discussion. The debate was on the question: Are the base church communities a new way of being church, or a new way for the whole church to be? Both views had their defenders, who presented arguments for the ecclesiological legitimacy of their position.

The best approach to a resolution of the question was, in my view, that outlined by the theologian and observer Clodovis Boff. He raised a number of important questions: 'Can it be that only the base church communities embody this new way of being church, or is there more to it? The new way of being church is greater than the base church communities.'[10] The path he traced to illustrate his position followed the route of articulating an understanding of the base church communities within the broader process of the church of the poor. While it still needs a more robust definition, the 'project-process' of a church of the poor is in the ascendant, representing 'more than just the phenomenon of the base church communities involving the structures of the "traditional church" as well, with its various authorities, and popular Catholicism, too. The base church communities have a role as protagonists within the whole.'[11] So the communities would be the engine, as it were, driving the process of wider church renewal, which involves the whole institution.

Clodovis Boff's contribution served to resolve a certain rigidity in ecclesiological analysis of the base church communities, also encouraging recognition of the special value and ecclesial relevance of other experiments taking place, which could also make a contribution to the base church communities. Such experiments are, together with the base church communities, involved in the wider project of a church of the poor, impelled by the call to the categorical imperative to follow Jesus. This reflection opened the gates to what I consider the best way of understanding the base church communities: their importance in this context is the strong summons they issue to the whole church by pointing to basic values of the kingdom and of following Jesus: conversion to solidarity with the impoverished, striving for the cause of integral liberation leading to an egalitarian society, and the evangelical affirmation of life.

There is no way of being church today without attending to this evangelical challenge. However, this does not mean that the base church communities are 'the way for the whole church to be', but simply that they embody a 'new way of being church' that calls the whole church to conform to the outlook of the church of the poor. The whole of traditional parish-based pastoral activity, as well as middle-class and other church movements, are challenged by this new form of being church. What is now required is a pastoral redefinition and a critical openness to activating a dimension that is constitutive of preaching the gospel, acting for justice and sharing in the transformation of the world.

II. Base church communities: a church in permanent genesis

Faced with the complex political situation in Brazil and the drawing-back of the church, the base church communities have been through a new learning process. The experiences they have undergone have also contributed to bringing new questions to the fore, questions that had not formerly been appreciated, or had been pushed to the background in view of the needs of the moment. Particularly since the late 1980s, the base church communities in Brazil have been experiencing greater challenges. A number of the dioceses that originally provided the space for the experiment have gone through a process of pastoral assessment (Vitória, Goiás, São Felix do Araguaia, Crateús, São Mateus, Volta Redonda).[12] These assessments have produced some startling results. Also, the inter-church meetings of the base church communities themselves have raised new questions and challenges for further reflection and creativity within the communities. The increasing engagement of militants from the base church communities in popular movements, trade unions and political parties has also produced new situations, forcing the communities to take a less boastful line.

This new stage on the journey of the communities, a stage for redefining their citizenship, might be called that of 'diminished certitude and increased investigation'. There is a new consciousness of the community as a living reality and one in a continual process of creation and re-creation, attentive and open to the new signs of the times, discovering untrodden paths and resistant to the temptation to see everything in simplistic terms of black and white. There is today a clear conviction that the history of the base church communities is an open history, not crystallized. There is no more space for idealistic reifications; it is time for a new feeling for the ways of reality.

We are now going through a new stage of examining the experience of the communities in the light of the new challenges being perceived, recognized and worked out within the base church communities themselves. Particular aspects of their situation are being singled out: new pastoral questions and 'knots' to be unravelled, challenges stemming from their previous course and their internal contradictions. The communities are therefore going through a new period of self-evaluation, in which the new questions raised are helping to perfect the experiment and to consolidate it in history and society.

To examine the whole complex of the challenges being faced by the base church communities today would produce an imbalance within the space of this article, which must remain a broad-brush picture. I shall therefore limit myself in this part to pointing out one or two of the particular challenges facing them in the latter part of the 1990s.

1. *The challenges of a deeper ecumenicity and the inter-religious dialogue*
The ecumenical spirit was present in the base church communities from

their inception, shown in a living way in the inter-church meetings which inspired the communities from the late 1970s, giving them a more precise understanding of their place in the church. The subject of ecumenism arose not as an originally explicit concern, 'but as the fruit of a rich biblical experiment carried out within the communities, and from working together in the social field, through movements reclaiming and defending human rights'.[13] In a certain sense, Latin America can be said to be offering the world, as its special contribution, a new ecumenism, born of common service to the mission of liberation. The urgency of this mission has made possible a new unity, in which the real differences have not stood in the way of a new form of living together.

The ecumenical dimension has been one of the chief concerns, particularly at the last two inter-church meetings, held in Caxias in 1989 and Santa Maria in 1992. At these, the presence of the evangelical churches became more vocal and effective. At Caxias, twelve ecumenical churches were represented, giving their witness through 120 of their members, men and women; at Santa Maria, the presence was maintained with 106 representatives. At both meetings, the evangelicals were present as either delegates, observers or guests. Their participation had a visible expression in the celebrations, in which non-Catholic bishops, and women and men pastors, took a leading part, reading the word of God, preaching, or blessing the faithful; the same was true of the statements and interventions made in plenary and group sessions, and in the various acts of prayer and symbolic expression.

But once this ecumenical dimension in the inter-church meetings, special events in the ecumenical life of the churches in Brazil, has been recognized, one has to point out that such experiences amount to more of a proclamatory and anticipatory sign than a situation calmly accepted and acted upon in the life of the base church communities. Tensions and resistance in this field can still be seen very much at work in some quarters.

Ecumenical feeling has lately been strengthened in the base church communities as a result of the challenge from other religions. Because they are rooted in the popular domain, the communities live cheek-by-jowl with other religious expressions current among the people, some of them vigorous, such as Pentecostalism and Afro-Brazilian religions. So the communities face a new challenge: how to work for a deep inculturation of a Christian faith capable of sustaining a fruitful and lively dialogue with these new religious expressions present among the people.

Recent experiences, including that of the latest inter-church meeting, have pointed to the need for a greater deepening of the ecumenical dimension of the communities, of the multi-cultural matrix of Catholicism in Brazil, of the dialogue between the Christian faith and Afro-Brazilian religions, and of the advances in inculturation in the liturgical, theological and pastoral fields. The actual experience of certain base church communities in living with particular forms of Christian inculturation, and of the double religious practices of some of their members, has raised extremely complex and challenging questions for the whole notion of inculturation. Some authorities have even stressed the importance of deepening and broadening the determinant principle of Catholicism itself, on seeing the practices current among some members of the communities. In very particular cases, a Catholic identity does not indicate or define an exclusive belonging. The learning process that takes place in a relationship of close proximity to the world of 'others' makes possible a 're-semantization' of one's own universe of meaning. This has led to a re-examination of syncretism as a positive value in certain community situations, as redefining the actual religious and social identity of community members.[14]

The emergence of the subject of inculturation in the base church communities had very deep repercussions on their life and their relationship with the church as a whole. While before, in the 1970s and early 1980s, it was the subject of faith and politics that brought tension and unease, the entry of this new question had an even more explosive impact. The emergence of reflection concentrating on the question of culture, particularly when this is a religious culture, brought out unknown or stifled forces. It is a subject that affects persons in the depths of their being, bringing out strong feelings; it also enables the question of authoritarianism in the exercise of church life to emerge more clearly.

It is not surprising, therefore, that realization and revindication of the rights of blacks, women and Indians should have exploded at the Seventh Inter-church Meeting, which tackled just this question of oppressed cultures. The right to have their social and religious citizenship recognized made itself felt at every step of the meeting, with its revindication now clear and strong. These are new questions and challenges; they break with the traditional paradigms of Western, white, male Catholicism, prompting the opening of new paths of inculturation in both liturgy and expression of one's personal faith.

2. The challenge of spirituality

The course of spiritual life in the base church communities has always been linked to the aim of following Jesus. The history of the communities has been permanently marked by the evangelical imperative to live out the radical nature of Jesus' plan. As experiments in being church, they are bearers of the 'dangerous memory' of Jesus, of his dream of a horizon of the full affirmation of life.

Following Jesus implies a triple movement: exodus, commitment and closeness. There is no true following without the integrated presence of these three essential elements. In the 1970s and early 1980s, the base church communities in Brazil stressed above all the dynamic of incarnation of faith, of breaking the barriers of individualism, and of 'going out' in the direction of the impoverished sectors of the population, committing themselves to their cause. The stress fell on the urgency of liberating practice, of embodying faith in the exercise of political solidarity. This dynamic impulse was put into action with a great deal of effort and generosity. The call to holiness was expressed in commitment in history: politics, was the *locus* of sainthood. There was a clear perception that there could be no spiritual life without historical life, without effective solidarity with the impoverished.

Increasingly, during the second half of the 1980s and as the paradigms of modernity entered into crisis, a new view emerged in the communities: the understanding of the need to deepen their common and personal experience of following as 'closeness' to the Lord. This understanding was deepened and generalized in popular pastoral practice in the 1990s, above all in the communities. What became evident was the need to live liberating practice with a particular spirit.

Their spirituality was now deepened as experience of grace, of a loving meeting with God, of intimacy with the Lord. This was an experience of integration, providing a special climate in which full and true meeting with one's fellows could take place. This new stage in the life of the communities does not mean denying their whole history, since their commitment to the cause of life remains paramount. The particularity emerging now, which is enriching their current experience, is the rediscovery of faith as 'autonomous greatness, as self-directed value, as gratuitousness'.[15] The experience of faith has its value not only as a function of the struggle: there is a gratuitous grace that is vital also for our fulfilment as persons.

For many agents and leaders, 'drunk on longing for history', the new dynamic experienced in the communities has uncovered a facet that overturns the logic of productivity and efficacy. They are discovering that, besides the goals of organization and conscientization, there should equally be an assured and special space for working on the personal dimension of faith, for intensifying the experience of community: space and time to 'work on oneself'. So a basic challenge remains for the base church communities to guarantee the necessary equilibrium between the political and mystical dimensions of faith – 'that Christian faith should remain turned, by its intrinsic imperative, to the "question of the poor" and that solidarity with the poor should remain, in the church, firmly welded to its bases of faith'.[16]

It is interesting to note that the present demand for spirituality is coming about at a historical moment characterized by the 'crisis' of the paradigms of modernity and the increasing emergence of new forms of subjectivity. Notable in this whole bubbling up of subjectivity in the communities is a reaction against the activism and 'massification' of the modernization process, which has also penetrated into pastoral work. Faced with a culture rooted in instrumental rationality, one which colonizes the dynamic of life, the emergence of subjectivity comes to signal a new dimension of human achievement, in which men and women no longer simply dominate the world, but seek above all a reason for living.

In the same movement of recognizing the singularity of the experience of 'closeness', the communities are rediscovering affectivity as a value in community life. They are learning that often, in the name of a historical 'urgency', they sacrificed subjectivity, and with it gratuitousness, affectivity and the symbolic world. Subjectivity is now demanding its space, its place. At the Santa Maria meeting, the women present above all raised this question or affirmed their right to respect in the church for their feminine identity and their commitment to the struggle for self-valuation of their own bodies, for the rediscovery of their sexuality and for a rebuilding of man-woman relationships.[17]

3. The challenge of presence in the masses

The challenge of missionary vitality and their place among the people is now one of the central concerns in the pastoral practice of the base church communities and in their reflection on experience. Their experience has, in effect, favoured work in small groups, the formation and qualitative deepening of people from the base of society in the affirmation of a new citizenship in society and in the church. The fact of belonging to one of these communities presupposes a 'conversion' in the way one experiences religion: that is, a certain level of advancement in and harmony with a more reflective 'dynamic' of living out one's faith. Such an experience does not come about without a certain rupture with the traditional patterns of religious experience found in the great mass of the people.

In the recent assessments of the pastoral situation of dioceses committed to the work of the base church communities it became clear that the number of Catholics effectively reached by the range of action of the communities was limited, since 'the most impoverished still play little part in the life of the church, or are not reached by its pastoral endeavour'.[18]

Research into this fact has been extended in the past few years, and it is now at the centre of concern, being also the overall subject for the next Inter-church Meeting of the base church communities to be held in 1997 in São Luis de Maranhão: 'Base Church Communities, Life and Hope in the Masses.'

The actioning and extension of this inquiry have thrown up particular problems: the great penetrative power of the Pentecostal movement among the masses, the distance and tension between the base church communities and traditional popular or privatized Catholicism, the huge areas beyond the outreach or insufficiently reached by the pastoral activity of the communities, and so on. This whole situation has provoked the major challenge for the communities of deepening their option for the most impoverished and excluded.

Either the communities accept the challenge to open out to the great mass of Catholics, or they will remain in the situation of being part of minority Catholicism within Brazilian society.[19]

They are accepting that it would be an illusion to imagine the whole church in Brazil as a 'great web of communities', but they are accepting the challenge to work toward a greater involvement with the mass of those excluded from society. They now have a more ready understanding of the real dimensions of this problem, and are paying closer attention to the subjects of popular religion, sacramental Catholicism, means of communication and other important aspects of mass pastoral concern. There is a search for a new approach to the methodology required for working with the masses and linking this to work in community.

This final challenge, like the two discussed previously, belongs within a broader spectrum of subjects that will engage the thought and activities of the communities in the coming years. They are new issues, but they certainly do not abolish or minimize the fundamental issue that has been with the communities since their inception: the affirmation of life and the evangelical option for the impoverished. Commitment to the cause of life and the social sphere has absolutely not been abolished. The quest today is for a way of achieving it within a new synthesis, in which the emergent issues can receive equal attention.

Translated by Paul Burns

Notes

1. R. Valle and M. Pitta, *Comunidades eclesiais católicas – resultados estatisticos no Brasil*, Petrópolis 1994. See also the commentary on the research: P. A. R.

de Oliveira, 'CEBs: o que são? Quantas são? O que fazem?' in *REB* 54, 1994, 931–4.

2. Oliveira, 'CEBs' (no. 1), 932.

3. E. Durham, 'Movimientos sociais: a construção de cidadania', *Novos Estados CEBRAP* 10, 1984, 28.

4. Letter from the Seventh Inter-church Meeting of Base Church Communities', in *REB* 49, 1989, 688.

5. Brazilian National Bishops' Conference, *Comunidades eclesiais de base na Igreja do Brasil*, São Paulo 1982, no. 78.

6. Cf. F. L. C. Teixeira, *A fé na vida*, São Paulo 1987, 192–3.

7. R. Valle and C. Boff, *O caminhar de uma Igreja nordestina: avaliação pastoral da diocese de Picos*, São Paulo 1993, 39–42.

8. See the significant testimony of Dom Alois Lorscheider, 'The Re-defined Role of the Bishop in a Poor, Religious People', *Concilium* 176, 1984, 47–9.

9. The question of the challenge of new ministries was the subject of the second meeting of the Episcopal Commission of the Brazilian National Bishops' Conference with representatives of the National Commission of Base Church Communities held in Brazilia in April 1995. Cf *Comunicado Mensal – CNBB* 490, 1995, 586–7.

10. C. Boff, in *Sedoc* 19, 1986, 488; id., 'En que ponto estão hoje as CEBs?', *REB* 46, 1986, 535.

11. Ibid., 488.

12. Most of these findings were assessed by the Assessment Team of the Institute for Studies in Religion (ISER) in Rio de Janeiro.

13. Brazilian National Bishops' Conference, *Comunicado Mensal* 482, 1994, 1230, on the first meeting between the Episcopal Commission and the National Commission of Base Church Communities, held in June 1994.

14. Cf P. Sanchis, 'O repto pentecostal a "cultura católica-brasileira"', in A. Antoniazzi et al., *Nem anjos nem demônios: interpretações sociológicas do pentecostalismo*, Petrópolis 1994, 48–9; id., 'Pra não dizer que não falei de sincertismo', *Cominicaçoes do ISER* 45, 1994, 7; J. B. Libânio, 'VIII Encontro Intereclesial das CEBs (eventos no evento)', *REB* 52, 1992, 794, 797.

15. C. Boff, 'Comunidades eclesiais de base e culturas', in F. L. C. Teixeira et al., *CEBs: cidadania e modernidade*, São Paulo 1993, 81.

16. C. Boff, 'Como vai a teologia da libertação' (pamphlet), Rio de Janeiro 1995, 8.

17. Final Document of the Santa Maria meeting, in *Sedoc* 25, 1992, 364.

18. Archdiocese of Vitoria – ES, *Opcões a diretrizes pastorais da Igreja de Vitoria*, São Paulo 1987, no. 59.

19. P. A. R. de Oliveira, 'Catolicismo de massa no Brasil: um desafio para as CEBs' (pamphlet), Rio de Janeiro 1995, 9–10; C. Boff, 'Os nós pastorais de igreja de Picos', in R. Valle and C. Boff, *O caminhar* (n. 7), 97–9. See also Brazilian National Bishops' Conference, *Diretrizes gerais da ação pastoral da Igreja no Brasil, 1991–1994*, São Paulo 1991, nos. 208, 219.

A Protestant Response

Miroslav Volf

If I have understood the ecclesiological parts of Harold Hunter's article correctly, the basic ecclesiological convictions of the world-wide Pentecostal movement which works as an 'amorphous mass' can be summed up as follows:

- *The local church is central,* because 'worship' – this 'sacred theatre of the Spirit possessed – stands in the centre of ecclesial life.
- *The structures of the church are pluriform,* since there is no 'single pattern of ministry which might serve as a blueprint' for all Pentecostal churches.
- *The life of the church is participatory,* since 'each member is expected to be active and carry the flame'.

In this article I shall presuppose the first two basic convictions and occupy myself more closely with just the third. In my view the real ecclesiological challenge of the Pentecostal movement for the Protestant churches lies in this third basic conviction. These churches must discover anew theologically and learn to live out anew today what they have already known and in part lived out from the beginning: the active priesthood of all believers, a priesthood which they originally understood not only soteriologically but also ecclesiologically.

But how is the church to be thought of as a dynamic, participatory and polycentric communion, whose life does not follow a simple monocentric-bipolar pattern – with the active bishop or pastor who commands at the centre and the receptive and obedient community on the periphery?[1]

I. The local church is central

The participatory-polycentric character of the church has a twofold theological basis: in the Christian call to faith and in the charism. Christians are called to enter into fellowship with Jesus Christ (I Cor. 1.9) and to confess and bear witness to him with words and actions (I Peter 2.9). They have been given authority and enabled for this ministry through initiation by the Spirit of God. The call to faith and ministry is universal, once-for-all and permanent. By contrast, the forms of ministry change, as do those who hold this ministry and the situations in which they find themselves. Therefore the call can only be the basis for a universal priesthood which is the same for all members of the church because it is not yet differentiated in a concrete way, not for the various changing ministries of each member.

The specific way in which each individual Christian fulfils his or her universal priesthood must be grounded by charisms specific to each individual – even if it is true that each Christian gets a specific charism (or charisms) in the universal call. For the charisms are what enable pluriform ministries in the church and the world, proceeding from the grace of God and (potentially) changing and overlapping. The relationship between call and charisms is to be defined as follows: the call to new life and to the doing of works in keeping with this life, which goes out to all without distinction through the word of the gospel, is made concrete in the individual appropriation of this call in the gifts of the Spirit which are given (or are to be given) to each individual for changing tasks in the church and the world which are specific to individuals.[2] *That* all Christians have a task in the church and the world is grounded in their Christian calling; *what* concrete ministry (or ministries) they have is determined by the gifts of the Spirit given to them at this point in time.

In accordance with their being called and endowed by the Spirit of God, all members of a church depict and offer the manifold grace of God through their actions and words (see I Peter 4. 10f.). All have to make a contribution in worship and in the whole life of the church.[3] The church comes into being and comes to life through the communication of salvation by mutual service with the pluriform gifts of the Spirit. However, not everyone takes part in the communication of faith in the same way and with equal intensity. Above all, we should not underestimate the outstanding importance of those who are 'in office'. They have an irreplaceable role in the church. But the whole life of the church is not ordered around them. Different people can be the soteriologically 'significant others' for different people. In addition to this, all members of the church create the 'plausibility structures' in which the communication of faith and life in faith first becomes possible. Thus the Spirit does not constitute the church exclusively through those who bear office, but through all members, who serve the others with their gifts.

II. The structures of the churches are pluriform

I shall now go on to attempt to define the polycentric-participatory model of church life more closely. First of all, however, I want to draw out briefly some practical consequences of this model.

This model first represents merely a reinterpretation of what actually happens in the churches. The current model, according to which the Spirit constitutes the church through those who hold office (ordained in the apostolic succession), leaves out the ecclesiologically very significant fact that in all churches faith is communicated and kept alive above all through the (so-called) laity – in families, among neighbours or at the workplace; without the activity of the laity in communicating faith there would be no living church. Ecclesiologically, it also underestimates the contribution of the laity in worship. In all churches they take part in worship by singing, praying, reading scripture, confessing the faith or even by their mere presence. Ecclesiologically, too, these activities must also be taken to constitute the church.

Theological reinterpretation of what in fact has always happened in the church is at the same time an important presupposition for a new church practice. For the ecclesiological omission of the role of the laity in constituting the church is one of the most important theological reasons for their passiveness. If they are constituted as the church by receiving the sacraments and/or hearing the word that is preached, then active participation in the communication of faith is external to their ecclesial being: they are the church in their passiveness; their activity is – or is not – additional to their being the church. By contrast, if the church is constituted by all its members, then the communication of faith is a dimension of their ecclesial being: they are the church in their activity of communicating the faith (though this is merely the other side of their receptive passiveness and is first made possible by this passiveness).

However, the passiveness of the laity has other than a merely theological basis. Sociological factors are particularly important (though architectural ones should not be forgotten either!). Following Max Weber and Ernst Troeltsch, Hervé Legrand rightly understands the tendency to disqualify the laity in religious terms partly 'on the basis of the necessary division of labour in any society . . . We see that the identity of the clergy is dialectically bound up with the religious dispossession of the laity (the "clergy" inculcate in the "laity" their lack of knowledge and power) and the symmetrical affirmation by the laity of its own election and its own superiority.'[4]

A first step towards countering this sociological tendency is a theological revaluation of the laity as the medium through which the church is constituted by the Spirit of God. I want to contribute to such a revaluation here by a brief reflection on some ecclesiologically relevant characteristics of the charisms.

III. The life of the church is participatory

First, as the church comes into being through the presence of Christ in the Holy Spirit, the thesis that the whole people of God, called and with charismatic gifts, constitutes the church, presupposes that the exalted Christ himself acts in the gifts of the Spirit. According to the Pauline understanding of charisms this is in fact the case. For as Ernst Käsemann emphasizes, a gift of the Spirit is 'the specific part which the individual has in the lordship and glory of Christ'.[5] For this reason, the charisms are not gifts which can be separated from the concrete presence of Christ in men and women, which could be disposed of freely. He himself is 'present, in his gifts and in the ministries which they exist and indeed make possible'.[6] Since, as we shall soon see, all Christians have charisms, Christ also acts through all members of the church, and not just those who hold office. Many churches have made this point critically in their official responses to the Lima document by saying that the text puts too much emphasis on the representation of Christ by the ordained ministry.

The second characteristic of the charisms is their universal distribution. According to the texts of the New Testament, charisms are 'a phenomenon not limited to a particular circle of persons, but quite universal in the church' (see I Cor.12.7; Rom. 12.3; Eph. 4.7; I Peter 4.10). In the community as the body of Christ there are no members without charisms. The Spirit which is poured out on all flesh (see Acts 2.17ff.) also distributes the gifts to all flesh. Therefore the division into those who serve the community and those who allow themselves to be served is ecclesiologically untenable: each person is to serve with his or her specific gifts, and each is to be served in his or her needs. But in the churches as they are, many members are passive. So while not every baptized person is already to be called a charismatic, the charisms are present in each 'in germ', as Karl Rahner puts it.[7] According to the degree to which individuals are given charisms (see I Peter 4.10) – there is no pressure towards activity – they are to be recognized, enlivened and used for service in the church and the world.

The universal distribution of the charisms implies shared responsibility for the life of the church. Shared responsibility is quite compatible with the particular charisms of leadership ('those in office'). However, in the context of the universal distribution of charisms this takes on a new profile. The task of the leaders – whether ordained or not – cannot be to do everything in the church. This would lead to a hypertrophy of this one member of the body of Christ, the other side of which would be the complete atrophy of all other members. It is their task to animate all members of the church to plurifom charismatic activities and to co-ordinate these. Secondly, the leaders are responsible for a church which has come of age, which is called to test every manifestation of the Spirit (see I Thess. 5.21).

The third characteristic of the charisms is their fundamental interdependence. All have charisms, but each person does not have all charisms. The fullness of gifts is to be found in the whole (local) church. In several passages Paul emphasizes that – according to their functions – the members of the body of Christ 'have different gifts' (Rom. 12.6; cf. I Cor. 12.7ff.). The church is not a club of universally gifted and therefore self-sufficient charismatics, but a community of men and women whom the Spirit of God has endowed in particular respects in order to be able to serve one another and the world in anticipation of the new creation.

As the members of the research are interdependent, their life must be characterized by mutuality. The church is a fellowship 'in [mutual] giving and receiving' (Phil. 4.15). The 'charisms of office' must be integrated into this mutuality. Those who hold office do not stand over against the church in acting exclusively as the person of Christ. Since the Spirit of Christ does not act in them by virtue of their office but in the act of exercising their ministry,[8] their action does not differ in principle from that of any other member of the church. In that all members contribute in their specific ways to various aspects of the life of the church, they act as Christ's representatives towards those to whom their action relates. This does not eliminate the unavoidable polarity between service in the person of Christ and service of the community. But it is seen in decentralized terms, and thus the bipolarity of 'person in office – community' is overcome. *Spiritual activity and receptiveness are no longer divided into two groups of persons but represent two basic activities of each individual: each individual acts in the person of Christ and each is a recipient of this action.*

Fourthly, the sovereign Spirit of God assigns the charisms as the Spirit wills (I Cor. 12.11). The Spirit works *as* the Spirit wills: the church – a whole (local) church or a stratum in the church – cannot prescribe which gifts the Spirit will give to which member. And the Spirit works *when* the Spirit wills: the church cannot define at what time the Spirit will give the gifts. This makes it clear that the church lives from a dynamic which does not come from itself. In an important sense the problem who has to do what in the church is not a church matter. The church does not organize its life; the Holy Spirit 'organizes' it. Thus the pneumatological structure of the church follows from the sovereignty of the Spirit in the bestowal of the charism. Certainly, the church is initially structured through the apersonal institutions: these need not be devised all over again with changing situations, but are already given. There are different more or less stable ecclesial ministries (like *episkope* and *diakonia*). But these institutions cannot be thought of without persons in them.[9] The personal structure of participation in these institutions is determined by the sovereign Spirit who distributes the charism to whom the Spirit wills, when the Spirit wills.

Fifthly, it is important to reflect how the charisms are given by the sovereign Spirit. They are often described as 'surprising' or 'eventful', so that one cannot do other towards the charisms than be 'available' for them – or not.[10] From this follows the contrast between charism and office: the charism is 'immediate' and 'outside human control'; the office can be handed down sacramentally. But this model of the distribution of the charisms is too simple. Paul calls for 'earnest desire' for the charisms (I Cor. 12.31; 14.1). This presupposes the assessment of one's own innate or learned capacities and the needs of the church; one must know what the others need and what one has or does not have oneself, in order to be able to serve them. However, I cannot simply seek out my charisma in accordance with my estimation of the situation. Striving for particular charisms makes sense only if I am prepared to allow my assessments of myself and others to be corrected by the assessment by others of me and of themselves. For the others must be willing to accept my service. This results in the interactional model of the distribution of charisms.[11] I acquire the charisms from the Spirit of God through interaction with myself – with what I am by nature and what I have become on the basis of my capacities in society – and through interaction with the church and the world in which I find myself. Charisms are gifts of the sovereign Spirit of God; however, the Spirit does not give them to the isolated individual, but to men and women in their concrete natural state and sociality. Precisely because they are gifts of the sovereign Spirit, the charisms are not primarily ecclesial in their orientation, but in their distribution.

Sixthly, the synchronic and diachronic plurality of the charisms is important for a participatory model of the church. According to Paul, any person can have several charisms at the same time. Granted, Paul does not know any universally gifted personalities who could live independently of the community. But in the framework of ecclesial interdependence he is concerned that each person should have the charisms 'in fullness' (I Cor. 14.12).

Diachronic plurality is even more important than synchronic plurality in relation to the structures of the church. In contrast to calling, the charisms – in the theological sense of calling to a particular service in the church and the world and the capacity to perform it – are not 'irrevocable' (Rom. 11.29). Several charisms can replace one another in the course of time. This is an implication of the interactional model of their distribution: with the history of the community and its individual members the charisms with which these serve in the community also change – particular charisms come to the fore at certain times and others become unimportant (either for the community or for those who have them). That does not mean that the divine calling and endowment for a ministry cannot be for life. But it need not be. At all events, there is no correlation between the permanence of a charism and its divine origin. The Spirit of God is the Spirit of life. That is why the Spirit's gifts are as varied and as dynamic as ecclesial life itself.

4. In his book on the 'church in pluralism', Michael Welker has recently called for the 'simple hierarchical and one-too-many structures which still stamp our churches' to be replaced by 'the development of new forms which make it possible for the community to have a share in shaping and putting its stamp on worship – including its content'.[12] Welker has rightly addressed his request, which corresponds to my attempt to overcome the monocentric-bipolar ecclesial structures and think of the church as a participatory, polycentric and dynamic communion, to the Protestant churches. But the Pentecostal churches should hear a warning in it, too.

Harold Hunter complains about 'the rise of bureaucracies and shibboleth monitors' in the Pentecostal churches. Nancy Bedford, who teaches theology in Buenos Aires, made the following observation there about the 'ethos' of some rapidly growing charismatic churches:

'It centres on following "spiritually gifted" *candillos* (largely male) who are both charismatic and authoritarian. Thus the form seems congregational but the ecclesiological substance reverts to the worst kind of priest-centred Catholicism . . . It is an example of the gospel adapting to a culture and growing (in some cases phenomenally) – but at what price!'[13]

Translated by John Bowden

Notes

1. For the basic features of a participatory ecclesiology which has been developed in the dialogue with Catholic ecclesiology (represented by Joseph Cardinal Ratzinger) and

Orthodox ecclesiology (represented by Metropolitan John Zizioulas), see M. Volf, *Die Kirche sind wir! Eine ökumenische Untersuchung über das Verhältnis von Trinität und Kirche*, Mainz 1966; see also J. Moltmann, *The Church in the Power of the Spirit. A Contribution to Messianic Eschatology*, London and New York 1977, 337ff.

2. For a brief theological reflection on charisms see M. Volf, *Work in the Spirit. Toward a Theology of Work*, New York 1991.

3. This is not to be understood as an implicit endorsement of the inappropriate criticism of liturgical worship which has become traditional in Free Church and Pentecostal circles, but as a plea to understand and shape the liturgy in a particular way.

4. H. Le Grand, 'La Réalisation de l'Église en un lieu', in *Initiation à la pratique de la théologie. Dogmatique* III, ed. B. Lauret and F. Refoulé, Paris 1983, 143–5, 184.

5. E. Käsemann, 'Ministry and Community in the New Testament', in *Essays on New Testament Themes*, London 1964, 63–94:65.

6. Ibid., 74.

7. K. Rahner, 'Charisma', LThK 2, 1025–30: 1028.

8. Cf. E. Schweizer, 'Konzeptionen von Charisma und Amt im Neuen Testament', in *Charisma und Institution*, ed. T. Rendtorff, Gütersloh 1985, 316–49: 331.

9. The ecclesiological distinction between apersonal institutions and the personal structure of participation corresponds to the sociological distinction between 'key roles' in a social system and 'allocation of human capacities and human resources among tasks' (T. Parsons, *On Institutions and Social Evolution. Selected Writings*, ed. L. H. Mayhew, Chicago 1982, 120). In addition a distinction must be made between institutions and persons on the one hand and the ministry which is exercised by persons through institutions on the other. Thus according to the Protestant understanding, ministry in the word of God is constitutive of ecclesiality, and particular institutions through which this ministry is exercised are not.

10. Thus N. Baumert, '"Charisma" – Versuch einer Sprachregelung', *ThPh* 66, 1991, 21–48: 32ff., 45.

11. Similarly also J. Veenhof, 'Charismata – Supernatural or Natural?', in G. Vandervelde (ed.), *The Holy Spirit: Renewing and Empowering Presence*, Winfield 1989, 73–91: 90f.

12. M. Welker, *Kirche im Pluralismus*, Gütersloh 1995, 125f.

13. Personal communication.

Healing and Deliverance

A Pentecostal Perspective

Cheryl Bridges Johns

For Pentecostals, healing and deliverance are constitutive aspects of the gospel. They are means whereby the 'good news' is proclaimed in both the physical and spiritual dimensions of reality. Such manifestations are reflections of the power of the gospel for the whole person and for the whole of the cosmos.

In this brief article I will first attempt to describe a Pentecostal understanding of healing and demonic deliverance as reflecting a particular world-view which allows for transformational encounters through which sin-sick souls find *shalom*; where people marked by abandonment, solitude and impotency find a community that, without conditions, accepts them as one of their own. This new reality is one in which the untouchables are touched, not only by human hands, but by the divine.

Secondly, I will attempt to show how Pentecostalism reflects a correspondence between the spirit and body, thereby avoiding the dualism so prevalent in modern forms of Christianity. Pentecostalism's retrieval of the primal tactile forms of religious expressions allows for the whole person to experience the gospel's power of deliverance. Thirdly, there will be some concluding remarks about the role of Pentecostal communities as zones of healing and liberation.

I. The Pentecostal world-view: God-centred, transrational

The textual reality created out of the Enlightenment is one which leaves little room for the existence of the supernatural. This 'age of reason' reduced reality to what can be explained and controlled entirely by human ingenuity. The human subject, as knower, reigns supreme in the effort to control or to master the universe. Such a vision of reality depends upon a world-view which may be identified as being mechanistic in analogy, reductionistic in method, disciplinary in research, deterministic in outlook, static in perception, entropic in direction, dualistic in practice and positivistic in determination of truth.[1]

On the other hand, Pentecostalism reads reality from the basis of an 'affective experience with God which generates an apocalyptic horizon. In this apocalyptic horizon the experience of God is fused to all other perceptions in the space-time continuum.'[2] Most would classify such a world-view as 'pre-critical'. However, 'para-critical' may be a more appropriate term. The Pentecostal world-view has existed in a liminal state, flourishing in the margins of the post-Enlightenment world-view. In these margins persons encounter epiphanies of the divine presence in much the same manner as that recorded in the Scriptures.

With the advent of the postmodern revolution, there is now an awakening to the dead-endedness of the Enlightenment vision. The 'epiphanies of darkness' which surround all knowing call for a radical re-visioning of reality.[3]

Windows are now being opened on the realms of reality which exist outside objective, scientific knowledge. There is a renewed interest in the manifestations of healing and the realm of the supernatural.

While Pentecostalism has affinities with the emerging post-modern world-view, there are some major differences which affect the way Pentecostals understand healing and the demonic. First, the Pentecostal world-view is God-centred. Jackie Johns observes that in Pentecostalism 'All things relate to God and God relates to all things. This fusion of God with the phenomenological does not collapse God into creation. Instead, it is a predisposition to see the transcendent God at work in, with, through, above and beyond all events.'[4] Secondly, a Pentecostal world-view is holistic. Pentecostals are inclined to think systemically, which causes them to view revelation as progressively unfolding and to see an interrelation of the ages. All events, past, present and future, are related to a single master plan of God which will be consummated at the second coming of Christ. Consequently, Pentecostals view time as a whole.[5] There is a fusion of past, present and future. Steven Land notes that in Pentecostalism 'space and time are fused in the prophetic reckoning created and sustained by the Spirit of the end. Here and now, there and then are telescoped and traversed by the Spirit . . . '[6] Healings and deliverance from the demonic powers of this age are fused with the biblical witness and the age to come in which all will be healed and restored. Thus, Pentecostals live in the tension of the already but not yet consummated kingdom.

Within this tension is the Holy Spirit who will fulfil all things, yet who searches the mysterious depths of the Trinity. Unlike the scientific world-view, which views the world as operating out of laws and principles, a Pentecostal world-view is God-centred, and thus is centred in mystery.[7] This mystery acknowledges that some are healed while others are not. It allows for the handicapped to be instruments of healing for others. It allows for the Pentecostal pilgrim to journey with God and in God while not fully understanding the ways and means of the journey. So Pentecostals can sing, 'We will understand it better by and by'.

A Pentecostal world-view is also trans-rational. For Pentecostals, truth is not limited to reason. The spectrum of knowledge includes cognition, affection and behaviour, each of which is fused to the other two.[8] To know God is experientially to encounter God. This encounter results in a transformation of the knower. Transformation may occur in many forms. It may occur as deliverance from the demonic. It may occur as the new birth to salvation. It may occur as healing. It may occur as sanctification of the affections. And it may occur as being filled with the Holy Spirit.

In the modern world-view the human subject reigns supreme, while in the post-modern revolution the human subject is dead or at least de-centred. In a Pentecostal world-view, however, the subject is slain. To be touched by God is to be radically de-centred and re-centred in God! Thus, Pentecostals testify to coming to a knowledge of God and encountering the mystery of the holy. This radical de-centring results in a reorientation of self and world. While others have characterized this reorientation as escapism, the opposite effect often occurs. Pentecostal testimonies reveal an attempt to mesh the realities of life with the reorientated vision of the world. They speak of healing and deliverance, but also of suffering and pain. Such testimonies can serve as means of 'decoding reality' in order to analyse it for further action and reflection. The subject becomes the object which is slain, and this in turn becomes the re-orientated subject. The human, therefore, is both a subject of history and the object of divine initiative.

While many believe that a Pentecostal world-view contains a fundamentalist understanding of Scripture, there are some major differences. First, the Bible is first and foremost a living book.[9] It is the Word of God. Because there is a co-joining of God's presence with God's Word, to encounter the Scriptures is to encounter God. The Holy Spirit is the critical agent of this encounter, meshing together inspiration and interpretation. Secondly, the Scriptures serve as a template for reading the world. 'It is in the light of Scripture that the patterns of life are recognized and woven into the divine-human narrative. In this manner the Scriptures facilitate the formation of visions (pre-analytic, affective dispositions) within the believer which are perceived to conform to the character of God.'[10] Thirdly, the Scriptures function as a link to God's people and God's presence in the world throughout the ages. This link facilitates primitivistic and futuristic purposes of the people of God.[11]

Finally, it should be noted that a Pentecostal world-view is one in which evil is a reality. Pentecostals know that indeed there are those epiphanies of darkness which surround all knowing. They have never been able to believe in the modern ideal of the progress of history and its corresponding mythology of the power of humankind alone to solve the problems of the world. For them, the world is in a fallen state in which the powers of evil inhabit the created order. The devil, who is the 'prince of this world', is a personal spirit-being who controls the powers of darkness. Much like the ancient church, Pentecostals are engaged in a holy war against the kingdom of darkness. This war is fought in the spiritual realm and does not consist of violence in the physical world. It is fought through the weapons of prayer and often involves fasting. Pentecostals believe that evil spirits may inhabit human beings who have given themselves over to the kingdom of darkness. Exorcisms are open confrontations in which the evil ones are cast out and persons rescued for the kingdom of Christ. They are delivered from the clutches of a kingdom which is even now in death.

Because of this understanding of the relationship between the spirit world and the physical world, Pentecostalism flourishes in places like South Korea where there is a history of shamanism; or in Brazil, where there is widespread belief in both folk Catholicism and in a spiritism of the existence of evil spirits, magical powers and miracles. Harvey Cox observes that in Africa the growth of the indigenous Pentecostal churches provides a setting in which 'the African conviction that spirituality and healing belong together is dramatically enacted'.[12]

II. Spirit-body correspondence

A second factor in Pentecostalism's understanding of healing and deliverance is the movement's emphasis on the correspondence between spirit and body. In his assessment of Pentecostal spirituality Land notes that:

Pentecostals had a total 'body life' of worship. The whole body responded and each person presented his or her body in receptivity and yieldedness to the Lord. Hands would be raised in praise and in longing for his coming as the clouds of heavenly glory descended upon them. Hands would reach out to touch Jesus and by his Spirit receive healing and help. Hands would clap for joy at the mighty and wonderful deeds and presence of God. Hands would clasp and clench as believers reverenced and 'held on' to God for a blessing. The right hand of fellowship would be extended to all those coming into full membership in the church. Bodies would sway in the heavenly breezes, seeking healing, needing encouragement or being set forth by the body for some particular ministry.[13]

In the ministry of healing there is the expression of the belief that salvation and healing are for the whole person. The laying on of hands and anointing with oil are means whereby Pentecostals give expression to this belief. As recorded in the Gospels, Jesus comes as the Great Physician, healing both sin-sick souls and physical sickness. His touch is one which brings *shalom*, restoring wholeness. Thus Pentecostals testify to being touched by Jesus and made whole.

The touch of the divine upon human flesh reveals the good news that even the most weak and despised are worthy to become tabernacles of God's glory. Thus, the outcasts become vessels of honour through which God makes known the mysteries of his kingdom. It is not uncommon to find persons in Pentecostal communities who are either mentally or physically handicapped being used by God to bring healing to others. Their hands become the hands of God and their touch reveals the power of God. Indeed this is a mystery!

It is often the aspect of spirit-body correspondence which creates the most opposition to Pentecostalism. It makes Pentecostal services seem 'out of control' and 'too emotional' for those whose lives appear to be in control and whose approach to God is primarily cognitive. Yet it is this correspondence which appeals to those who know that they are not in control, who are not privy to the humanizing effects of the Kantian rule of reason. These persons, who have nothing to lose, receive with open arms the embrace of God. The Pentecostal message is thus a stumbling block for some and a message of liberation for others. It gives voice to the inarticulate and reduces the speech of the articulate and power to babbling tongues. How embarrassing, and yet, how subversively powerful!

III. Healing communities

While Pentecostals have their share of individuals who are known for their healing ministries, it is more common to find healing and deliverance occurring among them within communities of faith. These communities are free spaces or zones of liberation created by the Holy Spirit. David Martin reworks the conception of Pentecostalism as a haven. He notes that these havens provide for the dispossessed 'a new cell taking over from scarred and broken tissue. Within these new cells, a "new faith" is able to implant new disciplines, re-order priorities . . . and reverse the indifferent and injurious hierarchies of the outside world.'[14] Pentecostal communities thus help persons to become re-created, made anew.

The 'one-anotherness' of Pentecostal communities is exhibited in corporate prayer in which each person with a need is prayed for and each person prays. Thus, people both give and receive. No one knows for sure who will pray the prayer of faith, and each person's prayer is important and needed. Often Pentecostals pray aloud together in what is known as concert prayer. Each person is to be an instrument played by the Holy Spirit. Some become instruments of healing, others instruments of prophetic word, still others of the various gifts of the Spirit. In this context, healing occurs as a natural part of coming together.

In conclusion, it should be noted that Pentecostalism is a multi-facted movement. It is a global movement in which there is a great deal of diversity. However, these remarks about Pentecostalism's understanding of healing and deliverance are intended to reflect some of the broad consensus regarding these issues. It can be said that wherever the movement is flourishing, persons are finding deliverance from the powers of darkness and they are experiencing healing in both body and spirit.

Notes

1. These characteristics of the 'classical scientific world-view' have been outlined by Timothy Lines, *Systemic Religious Education*, Birmingham, Alabama 1987.

2. Jackie Johns, 'Pentecostalism and the Postmodern Worldview', *Journal of Pentecostal Theology* 78, 1995, 87.

3. See Charles Winquist, *Epiphanies of Darkness: Deconstruction in Theology*, Philadelphia 1986.

4. Johns, 'Pentecostalism' (n. 2), 88.

5. Ibid.

6. Steven J. Land, *Pentecostal Spirituality: A Passion for the Kingdom*, Sheffield 1993, 98.

7. Only recently, with the advent of the so-called 'health and wealth gospel', has there been an understanding within Pentecostalism of universal laws and principles of healing and prosperity which in a cause and effect manner bring healing to all who understand how to operate the system. This understanding is contrary to most classical Pentecostals' vision of reality, and reflects the influence of a simplistic 'modern' world-view.

8. Johns, 'Pentecostalism' (n. 2), 89.

9. Ibid., 90.

10. Ibid.

11. Ibid.

12. Harvey Cox, *Fire From Heaven: The Rise of Pentecostal Spirituality and the Reshaping of Religion in the Twenty-first Century*, Reading, Mass. 1995, 247.

13. Land, *Pentecostal Spirituality* (n. 4), 113f.

14. David Martin, *Tongues of Fire: The Explosion of Protestantism in Latin America*, Oxford 1990, 284.

The Response of Liberation Theology

Virgil Elizondo

Since 1968 I have been fascinated, enriched and encouraged with the empowerment of the poor which has taken place throughout Latin America with the expansion of the basic Christian communities and throughout the United States with the expansion of the community organizing groups. It is an incredible miracle of the Spirit to witness the coming to life of peoples who had previously lived a death-like existence as, in the power of their newly discovered status as children of God, they assume individual and collective responsibility for the betterment of their personal lives and that of their communities. The silent now become eloquent spokespersons and the 'ignorant' now exhibit forms of knowledge which are truly astounding. It is truly a new Pentecost. Reflecting on the inner meaning of these experiences of faith has given rise to what we know today as the theologies of liberation – theological reflection which has accompanied the people in their faith-inspired struggles for dignity, survival, justice and life.

I. Religious manifestation for minorities

In the last few years, I have been equally enthused by the growth and development of the Pentecostal movement, which is totally independent and different from any of the main-line churches: Protestant or Catholic. It erupted in 1906 in a prayer meeting in an old and run-down warehouse in Los Angeles conducted by an unemployed Afro-American which brought together poor whites, Afro-Americans and Mexican-Americans. It was probably the very first truly inter-racial prayer meeting ever held in the Americas. It did not depend on any doctrines, creeds or previous traditions, but simply on the immediate experience of God and the healing, liberating and empowering effects which this experience produceb in the individual participants.

This type of spomtaneous Pentecostal experience is often the only religious manifestation for minorities who lack access to the official ministries of the main-line religious structures. The poor and marginalized whom the ministers of the churches had served but kept powerless and undignified now assumed the dignified positions of minsterial leadership – especially the women and academically uneducated! The ones who had always been spoken to now spoke out for themselves; those who had never been authorized by church leadership now became the new authorities of the Spirit. They were healed of their academically imposed ignorance and delivered from their bondage to ecclesially ordained ministers. It was a unique moment of grace in which those who had been considered nothing by society and without any type of theological preparation, ecclesial ordination, or church backing gave birth to the fastest growing movement within the Christian family. Not only did they have a totally new experience of 'church', but they dignified and sanctified their separation from the established churches, which they judged as false and overly concerned with what they considered humanly-made dogmas and traditions. It is estimated that by the year 2000, one out of every four Christians will be a Pentecostal.

Some see opposition between Pentecostalism and liberation theology. Some have even said that as the church made an option for the poor, the poor made an option for Pentecostalism! I personally see both as powerful manifestations of the Spirit. They definitely differ in some very fundamental wkys, but are not really opposed, and are definitely not contradictory. In fact, each one has what the other one lacks and needs in order truly to accomplish its goals. Both empower the disenfranchised: Pentecostalism through interior deliverance of the individual and the liberation movements by enabling the people to take control of the forces of society which govern their destiny.

II. Origins of liberation theology and Pentecostalism

Liberation theology started among the dominant of society, who realized that the church, by the very nature of its origins, identity and mission, needed to be not only among the poor, but the church of the poor. The entire biblical message is the dangerous memory of the poor and a marginalized struggling for recognition, identity and new life. The pastoral agents and theologians who have been delivered from the allurements and blindness of the dominant world-view, while becoming very conscious of the unjust misery of the masses of the people, are the primary agents of the liberation movement, although they are the first to confess that it is when the poor themselves become empowered and the main agents of the movement that integral liberation will begin to take place. Thus it is the movement of the dominant, non-marginalized and non-poor at work among the poor, the powerless and the marginalized of society to awaken in them their God-given dignity, creativity and power. Through faith, knowledge and skills it seeks to transform the present world order of sin into a closer expression of the kingdom. The poor, with the help of the non-poor who are now in solidarity with them, are beginning to assume responsibility for their lives and work for a new creation.

There is no doubt that in analysing the root causes of the all-embracing oppression of the masses – of their depression, sadness, diseases, sicknesses, malnutrition and early deaths – the economic forces which maintained the social and political structures of oppression in place and even legitimized them emerged clearly as one of the chief concerns of the theologians of liberation. As time goes on, other forces of oppression and sickness are being identified and dealt with, such as ethnocentrism, racism and sexism. The naming of the 'idols' of the dominant structures of oppression has been one of the main sources of healing and deliverance within the movements of liberation. One of the critiques of Pentecostalism from within the movements of liberation is that often they perform exorcisms, but do not seek to name the specific demons of society which are producing the illness, thus giving the individual a personal experience of deliverance without seeking to eradicate the demon itself. Unless the roots of the disease are attacked, it will certainly continue to destroy people.

Pentecostalism erupted among the poor, marginalized and powerless themselves. In the context of prayer, these experienced the empowerment of the spirit of God, and like the very first Christians after Pentecost started with great joy, conviction and enthusiasm to share their experience with others. Nobody had to tell them they were to be missioners – the very spiritual power of their experience propelled them immediately to take their spiritual experience beyond their boundaries, and beyond any boundary. They did not have to wait for ecclesial or academic certification, for they were acting under the authority of the highest of all authorities: the Holy Spirit. They were no longer ashamed of being poor, uneducated, Black, Brown or White, for they had been reborn children of God. This experience gave rise to spontaneous sounds (tongues) which were like the cries of joy of a newly born child; it brought about healings as the 'untouchables' of society touched one another in faith. In the Pentecostal prayer meeting, everyone is welcomed and upon the reception of the Spirit is free to speak out, proclaim and sing the glories of God he/she has experienced. The great and unconditional freedom of expression is in itself healing and liberating for those whom society has convinced that they cannot speak well, that they are not sufficiently educated to express themselves properly, or that they do not have the proper authority to speak out.

III. Core themes and differences

At first sight, there is certainly a great similarity in the core themes of both Pentecostalism and liberation theology: the liberation which is experienced through following Jesus, the freedom and joy which one experiences in the kingdom of God, and the importance of institutional change, that is, of redeeming the world (the domain of Satan) for Christ. Both Pentecostalism and liberation theology are very aware (much more so than the theologies of the Enlightenment) of the wholistic stronghold of the powers of evil which blind and enslave persons, institutions and entire worldviews, and of the need for God to make a breakthrough.

The differences are more of emphasis than real differences. One of the major differences is in the notion of time. Whereas liberation theologies emphasize God's eruption in society in the here and now, Pentecostalism emphasizes God's eruption in the final apocalyptic coming of Christ at the end of time, which it tends to see as very near. Hence whereas liberation theologies sometimes appear to be too concerned with the affairs and forces of this world, Pentecostalism often appears to be exclusively concerned with the invisible, other-worldly powers which enslave persons and make them sick. One appears to be too worldly, while the other appears to be totally non-worldly. Yet upon closer analysis, it is evident that liberation theologies are deeply concerned with liberation from sin, conversion and the experience of God, while Pentecostalism is gradually becoming more and more aware of the social forces of evil working throughout society.

Whereas liberation theologies tend to begin when the poor become critical of the social and historical causes of their oppression and thus make great use of the critical analysis of reality so as to initiate change, Pentecostalism begins with the personal experience of being radically accepted, appreciated and valued by the community of God's people. Liberation theology begins with a rational faith conviction that leads to progressive experiences of God, while Pentecostalism begins with the trans-rational and transformative experience of God – being slain – which gradually leads to a new rational understanding of person, society and world.

Liberation theology simply assumes the need for personal conversion and prayer while placing the emphasis on the immediate transformation of society. In the beginning, it certainly was over-optimistic about the ability to transform the structures of evil into structures of the kingdom. Today, it is much more realistic in introducing such themes as survival, accompaniment and the crucified peoples. It is not abandoning the need for integral liberation but becoming much more aware of the complexity of the process – a process which will progress slowly and through great pain and sacrifice until the end of time. During this time, the need for the personal spirituality of the cross is becoming more central to liberation theology, as is evident in the present-day works of Gustavo Gutiérrez, Jon Sobrino, José Oscar Beozzo, Miguez Bonino and others. Yet deliverance/liberation from sin and the healing which comes through membership of the kingdom continue to be the very core of the Christian community movement and the theologies of liberation.

On the other hand, Pentecostalism, which had placed the emphasis on the immediate deliverance/liberation and transformation of the person and because of its emphasis on the apocalyptic end of the world ignored the immediate social order, is today realizing the need to become critically involved in the deliverance from evil of the various institutions of the world. Works like those of Cheryl Bridges Johns and Edwin Villafañe are bringing into centre focus the need for the reborn Christian to become critically involved in the transformation of the unjust social structures which condemn not only individuals but entire peoples to live and struggle in the dehumanizing conditions of misery caused by Satan as institutionalized in the structures of the present world order. However, as Cheryl Bridges Johns points out (p. 51, n. 7 above), the 'gospel of health and wealth' is gaining much popularity and strength throughout Pentecostalism, often turning the original movement of God's poor into big-business ventures and conservative political movements which ignore the social ills of society and even discredit the movements of the poor. Rather than working to change the world of sin from which they were delivered, they join it and actively participate in it for their own material enrichment, ignoring the impoverishment of others.

Both Pentecostalism and the theologies of liberation are about healing and deliverance. Both define and approach the devastating realities of individual persons and entire societies from different perspectives and different foundations, yet both are concerned with the kingdom of God becoming more of a reality among us. Both are just beginning with the two-thousand-year tradition of Christianity, but there is no doubt in my mind that they will be the two major manifestations of the Spirit in the Christianity of the third millennium.

Spirit and Body: A Feminist Response

Elisabeth Moltmann-Wendel

The phrase 'spirit and body' arouses a variety of feelings among Christians. First, Paul wrote of the body as the temple of the Holy Spirit, thus emphasizing a clearly positive relationship between spirit and body. At the same time, however, 'body' is indissolubly connected with 'flesh', and the apostle clearly had difficulties with that. 'In my flesh dwells no good thing . . . ' For many people, above all for women, yet a further problem is connected with this: the dualism of body and soul which entered theology and the church with Greek thought. The self identified itself with spirit or soul, and the body was calumniated and repressed. Now the calumniation of the body was in practice synonymous with the suppression of women. While the man identified himself with spirit, women were fixed to the body and nature.

How can a relationship to the Spirit of God be produced from these diffuse notions of body and spirit? First of all, it seems important to me to clarify the understanding of body within feminist theology and feminism, and then investigate its relationship to the Spirit.

I. The disclosure of the soul-body dualism

Feminist theology more than any other theological current has disclosed the dualism of soul and body which is open or concealed in theology, and demonstrated the specific places where this split comes about. It is women who have been made invisible and discriminated against in a long history, who have been reified in their bodies and made objects of desire and hatred. Violence against women, sexual exploitation and attacks of the kind that are becoming manifest today in all societies have shown once again how little success there has been in accepting women as having equal rights and their bodies – indeed human bodies generally – as God's good creation.

Theological women's research has shown the origins of this fatal tradition, which did not begin with Christian history but, after initial patterns of equality and wholeness in the life of the Jesus movement and early Christianity, very soon found fertile ground in Christianity. The conservative ethos which is already evident in the household tables of the New Testament; the influence of Stoic social ethics, which saw the goal of procreation not in pleasure but in reproduction; the repudiation of holistic Hebrew thought patterns; and the adoption of Aristotelian-dualistic notions were stages towards a religious dualism legitimated by Christianity. This was changed little even by later critical interventions – for example with Hildegard of Bingen. Women were identified with nature and body, and that made it possible to stylize them as mothers and saints, though at the same time – because of their own bodies, which were incalculable and fearful, they were seen as seductresses, as weak and to be feared, and despised as whores. In the Western tradition women's bodies were vessels which man claimed to fill, to dominate and to possess.

According to Jewish-Christian tradition, God's Spirit was to be poured out on all flesh, all bodies, as the prophet Joel, the Acts of the Apostles and texts of early Christianity imagined. The Spirit was to seize men and women without distinction of race, class and sex and develop a variety of capacities and functions in them. But as the church later became institutionalized, the Spirit became chained to the ordained ministry and thus to the man. Being filled with the Spirit, the characteristic of early Christianity, was replaced by the hierarchical order of the church, which eventually excluded women from all important office. Time and again throughout church history there were movements in which women claimed to be filled with the Spirit and justified by the Spirit to speak. But they, too, were constantly suppressed again or ultimately incorporated into a hierarchical order. Here mistrust of women and their bodies plays a role. The tabus which had been done away with in the Jesus movement and parts of the early church returned. The levitical laws of purity that affected women's bodies, which had lost their validity along with other laws of cleanness regulating diet and contact with the dead, reappeared. The consequence was that not only women's souls and bodies, but also the spirit and the body, became involved in an ongoing ecclesiastical controversy.

Present-day analyses and observations of the female body within patriarchal society show its reification. They point to its dependence on men, male norms and a Western value-system: women's bodies serve ideals of beauty determined by others, have to show forms and dimensions controlled by norms, serve as a cult object and a religious metaphor, and above all are always regarded as controllable and capable of adaptation. The analyses of violence against women which have been made in recent years – through incest, rape in marriage and on the streets, forced pregnancy in the war in Bosnia – are serious. But even medicine, which really should feel an obligation to the human body, seems still trapped in old patterns of domination: the woman's body has become a public place into which all scientists look without ceremony, and without preserving its mystery.[1] In *in vitro* fertilization the woman's body is quite simply compared with tubes and ampoules, i.e. vessels, which have to serve as material vehicles for the male seed which gives the form, and as a place where it is to be preserved.

II. The main conflict: unjust structures

However, for feminist theology, which seeks to help women all over the world to have respect for themselves and take responsibility for themselves, the conflict between self and body is only a secondary conflict within a greater conflict. For feminist theology, the main conflict is between the unjust structures of racism, sexism and classism and the claim of the message of the kingdom of God. Discovering this conflict and working to remove it is a social task. The rediscovery of wholeness in heaven and earth, immanence and transcendence, soul and body, nature and technology, is the vision which moves feminist theology. But this vision is still far from being achieved. Wholeness presupposes the overcoming of the roots of dualistic theology. The healing of the world is the programme of feminist theology, and this healing is not an individual but a social task. In it women see themselves as midwives who want to help to bring to life a society which allows, encourages, confirms and indeed blesses difference. The liberated body, the body which is no longer split off from the soul, the body which is moved by the Spirit, is therefore merely a vision on the periphery of a great process of healing.

Only a renewal and healing of the earth, only a social change in unjust structures, can ultimately free the bodies of women. In many feminist schemes, body has developed from an individual category into a social category. Therefore islands of such renewals are also to be thought of above all in collective terms: women's collectives, as Frigga Haug imagines them, in order to try out walking upright; the women's church, which fulfils this function in feminist theology. Communities are necessary for remedying social damage.

III. Women's insights into the body

But within feminism and feminist spirituality, women's insights into the body have also come into being which are undermining the hardened patriarchal structures and making individual new beginnings possible. They have also become important for feminist theology.

First, as women's bodies are measured by male capacity for achievement, male strength, continuous achievement, potentiality for commitment, women have begun to discover their own criteria of value. Here the woman's body, which is usually regarded as weaker than the man's body, unstable and susceptible, becomes a flexible medical wonder, capable of tremendous change, whose wounds e.g. at birth heal amazingly quickly. Its alleged passivity in conception has been proved to be a biological error. Women today can free themselves from false medical attributions, recognize their own values and live in accordance with them.

Secondly, the psychological investigations of Anne Wilson Schaef show a highly independent picture of women's bodies. Here healing is a process which takes place with the support and help of the healer in the sick person, whereas in the male pattern healing comes as a stimulus from outside.[2] So healing does not need any authorities, but rather helpers who seek to free the vital energies and support the process of self-healing.

Thirdly, in the woman's body a primal knowledge can be disclosed and vital energies can be regained which were held back under false attributions. Instincts can be aroused which were crippled in a one-dimensional rational culture of domination. The individuality and originality which is in every person, and which was hidden under a cover of anxiety, passivity and ignorance, can be opened up. Self-awareness and self-determination can shape a woman's body. Moreover self-determination of the body can also free people from ideologies old and new.

Moreover, such knowledge of the body and such healings of it can also be understood as political processes which dissolve the dualism on earth. The development of healing powers is necessary for our survival.

Many of these notions come from the matriarchal spirituality in which the goddess is seen as the power indwelling us, who with her vital energy sustains the cosmos. Such a picture of the goddess teaches women to see 'themselves as divine, the aggressions as healthy, their bodies as holy'.[3]

Traces of such notions also appear in feminist theological thought, as when 'grace and being in God indwell human nature itself'.[4] This happens when energies which slumber in people are aroused and mobilized. That came about when the Korean theologian Chung Hyun Kyung at the General Assembly of the World Council of Churches in Canberra drew a parallel between the Holy Spirit, which she mostly called 'she', and the East Asian Ki or Chi, the cosmic breath of life. (Ki or Chi is to be compared with the original Platonic Eros in the West.) From her women's base community, she brought to Canberra the message: 'Tell them not to use too much energy invoking the Spirit, for the Spirit is already here with us. Do not disturb the Spirit with your constant invocations. She is already strongly at work among us. The only problem is that we do not have eyes to see her and ears to hear her, because we are preoccupied with our greed . . . So tell them to repent.'[5]

IV. Rediscovering traditions

However, in addition to such matriarchal parallels, there are notions in the Christian, biblical tradition, rediscovered by women, which bring the spirit and body very closely together, and provoke new reflection on the relationship between spirit and body.

First, the New Testament stories of the healing of women in which Jesus is the integrating figure, since 'he tore apart the body-soul dualism by accepting women as they were, including their bodies'.[6]

Secondly, the Holy Spirit as woman and mother. The Indian Leelamma Athyal says of her: 'The Holy Spirit is the Mistress and Giver of Life, and the woman co-operates with her in so far as she plays an important role in the development of life.'[7]

Thirdly, the images of the church as body: 'Not the soul or mind or the innermost Self but the body is the image and model for our being church.'[8]

However, the story of Jesus and women, the female spirit which gives birth, the church as body of Christ, are hardly realized ideas through which we can overcome our hesitation to see spirit and body concretely together.

Mary Grey's reflections on Spirit, which is not hierarchical, not other-worldly, and which does not quench the person, are helpful. The Spirit embraces the body, changes it, gets the organs working and develops creative and productive power. It is characteristic of this understanding of Spirit that it does not work alone in a mysterious way but does something *with* us: shares in creating, forming, administering or being made visible through process and movement. Spirit creates communication in hearing and listening. It encourages the dumb,[9] the unheard, the formless, and brings it into existence. As early as 1974, one of the earliest feminist theologians, Nelle Morton, said: 'We experience God's Spirit as one who teaches people to listen. The word came and comes as human word, human expression of humanity. The creative act of the Spirit does not consist in making words resound, but in making the word, the breath and the language of creation heard. This experience is had where the Spirit is present in the community and moves the Pentecostal tongues of fire. It is present in the community and does not depend on a star, an expert or the technical knowledge which a hierarchical structure promises to an individual . . . We learn to hear with the whole body, to hear with the eye, to see with the ear, and to speak with the hearing, because we know that the Spirit is present, in a dynamic and not a static way.'[10]

The Spirit needs the body, but it throws it into confusion: the eyes which are used to seeing, hear; the ears, which are used to hearing, see: our well-adjusted body is thrown into fruitful disorder. Moreover the Spirit creates wholeness, binds physical, sexual and psychological life together. In it people become whole, and with the Spirit they are done justice to in their wholeness. All our separations and splits, conditioned by culture, are transcended but not levelled out. However, at the same time any 'spiritualization' is rejected. The totality of a person includes his or her social situation, as woman, as man, as coloured, as white, as handicapped. But wholeness also includes our becoming aware once again of our involvement in the cosmos and our being made fruitful by it.

And finally, Spirit touches us in the innermost part of our being, 'at the level of the archaic and instinctive, and brings the playful, joyful and ecstatic to life . . . ' In this connection Mary Grey refers to the charismatic movement, which emphasizes 'prophecy, spontaneity and joy in the Spirit, and the freedom of speaking with tongues'. Here office and Spirit are uncoupled.

So the Spirit brings to light new dimensions of our being and binds people together in an unaccustomed way. Here the Spirit touches human bodies very deeply. Spirit and body come together in these reflections. The body is now no longer scorned, made invisible and feared. It is seen again as God's creation in its deepest experiences, in its cosmic relationship and its unseen capacities.

In feminist theology the place of such new experiences is the women's church, the counter-culture to the patriarchate. Here wounds which have been inflicted in rape, through violence, sickness and incest, are healed. Here mourning is made possible, the hidden streams of energy are motivated, and healing is promised by the group. Here liberation from control by others and oppressive structures is celebrated, so that the true relationship to our physical reality, to the body, the earth and the divine is restored. Healings and even exorcisms are an old way to the Spirit which has been opened up anew. Healing can also take place in a new encounter with the Bible, where self-respect and dignity for women are again demonstrated by stories, and where mourning and rage at what has been missed have their place. The way for the Spirit is opened up in rituals and communities, and the oneness of spirit and body are brought to life. The church's reality is still far from such reconciliation and needs healing initiatives. But here already God and body meet, and Spirit and body find their place.

Translated by John Bowden

Notes

1. For the following see Elisabeth Moltmann-Wendel, *I am My Body*, London 1994 and New York 1995.

2. Anne Wilson Schaef, *Weibliche Wirklichkeit*, Wildberg 1985, 154.

3. Starhawk, 'Witchcraft as Goddessreligion', in C. Spretnak, *The Politics of Women's Spirituality*, New York 1982.

4. Rosemary R. Ruether, *Unsere Wunden heilen, unsere Befreiung feiern*, Stuttgart 1988, 103.

5. See Elisabeth Moltmann-Wendel (ed.), *Die Weiblichkeit des Heiligen Geistes*, Gütersloh 1995, 176f.

6. Aruna Gnanadason, *Die Zeit des Schweigens ist vorbei*, Lucerne 1993, 116.

7. Leelamma Athyal, 'Frauen und die Lehre vom Heiligen Geist', in Moltmann-Wendel (ed.), *Die Weiblichkeit des Heiligen Geistes* (n. 5), 165.

8. Elisabeth Schüssler Fiorenza, *In Memory of Her*, New York and London 1983, 380.

9. Mary Grey, 'Wohin flieget die Wildgans?', in Moltmann-Wendel (ed.), *Die Weiblichkeit des Heiligen Geistes* (n. 5), 143f.

10. Nelle Morton, 'Auf dem Wege zu einer ganzheitlichen Theologie', in E. Moltmann-Wendel (ed.), *Frau und Religion. Gotteserfahrungen im Patriarchat*, Frankfurt 1983, 208f.

Tongues and Prophecy

A Pentecostal Perspective

Frank D. Macchia

During the crucifixion scene of our church's Easter cantata, the choir sang a moving chorus about the love of Christ revealed in the cross. A dramatic pause followed the song. Suddenly, in the midst of the pause came a loud cry in tongues from a woman somewhere in the auditorium. She followed with a series of cries in tongues, which were not spoken as much as they were wept. The crucifixion scene had obviously moved her to an overwhelming sense of personal sorrow or grief. Her cries died down and were followed by another moment of silence as the congregation waited patiently for someone to clarify the meaning of what had just occurred. I am sure that most of us there had some sense of what the woman felt, revealing the capacity of language to engage others on a level deeper than cognitive understanding. An awesome sense of the divine presence was felt in that pause.

An interpretation came forth from a man seated near to us. He quoted several scripture passages verbatim relating to the meaning of the crucifixion in the light of the victory of the resurrection. It was by no means a translation of the tongues, since no words were adequate to capture fully those glossolalic cries. The interpreter functioned more like a critic who struggles to interpret a work of art. The interpreter also elaborated on those tongues by explicating their theological context. The interpretation that followed revealed that the woman was not just involved in sharing her own personal sense of sorrow or grief but that her glossolalic cries were also taken up in the much larger mystery of the redemption drama of Christ's death and resurrection and of the final redemption to come. The interpretation not only captured the meaning of the tongues but answered them. In concert with the interpretation, those glossolalic cries resounded with the sorrow and hope of a world waiting for God.

I. Tongues as *prodigium*

Tongues accent the inadequacy of language in the face of the awesome mystery of God. In focusing on this mystery, Pentecostals are drawn to the great theophany of God on the Day of Pentecost that involved a *prodigium* (an outstanding sign) of tongues of fire, understood by a number of Diaspora Jews from many lands, and the sound of a mighty wind (Acts 2.1–13). This theophany recalled Sinai (Ex. 19) and other theophanic encounters with God, particularly those that involved ecstatic prophecy as a sign of God's mighty and free self-disclosure (Num. 11).[1] The Pentecost theophany also fulfilled the decisive self-disclosure of God in Christ's death and resurrection (2.25–33) and anticipated the final theophany of God with 'blood, and fire, and billows of smoke' in the Day of the Lord (2.19–21). Tongues for Luke were the prominent sign of an eschatological theophany of God.

Tongues dramatize an encounter with God that is filled with awe and wonder. As such, tongues can help to renew our worship. Jacques Ellul complained that too many Christians are 'vaguely, tritely accustomed to God'. He asked, 'If prayer is indeed a speaking with God face to face, how could we remain forlorn inmates of commonplace?'[2] Similarly, Kenneth Leech complained that in worship there is a gradual 'decay of symbols, those powerful mysteries which swallow us whole, and through which we gain insights beyond words. There is a loss of wonder.'[3] It is precisely in response to such a loss of wonder that William Samarin described glossolalia as a 'linguistic symbol of the sacred' that is 'sacramental', announcing that 'God is here'.[4]

Viewing tongues as an encounter with the eschatological Spirit that is both spontaneous and 'sacramental' can move us occasionally beyond the impasse Paul Tillich noted in the struggle between the Protestant (especially Reformed) accent on the sovereign freedom of the Spirit and the Catholic emphasis on sacramental visible/audible means of grace.[5] Tongues can complement the liturgy to form an overall dramatic response to God which is ultimately too deep for words,[6] but which grants an equal role to both spontaneous and structured worship. Tongues can also function as the 'cathedral of the poor', defying the 'tyranny of words' in worship and dismantling the privileges of the educated and the literate, allowing the poor and the uneducated to have an equal voice.[7] As Krister Stendahl noted, there is an honourable place for ecstatic tongues in the church.[8]

Consequently, tongues have ecumenical significance, functioning in Acts as the decisive sign that connected the Gentile experience with that of the earliest Jewish Christians (10:46; 11:15).[9] The eschatological nature of this astounding sign of Pentecost is revealed partly in the fact that the ecumenical significance of the event begins, but is by no means completed, on the Day of Pentecost. The crowd that was so astounded by the miracle of tongues only represented Diaspora Jews; for instance, the so-called list of languages in Acts 2, the majority of which are provinces and lands, seems to have been selected because of the large Jewish population of each location.[10] The story of Acts reveals that the people of God must struggle toward ecumenism and catholicity. The ecumenical significance of glossolalia will not be fully realized until the final gathering of the people of God before God's throne (Rev. 7.9–10). As Russell Spittler stated, tongues are 'a broken speech for a broken body of Christ until perfection comes'.[11] Tongues are a sign of our brokenness and a foretaste of healing. Tongues express both the struggle and the hope, the tears and the joy. Tongues resist the claims of a realized eschatology that takes catholicity for granted and of a radical sectarianism that denies the scandal of the church's cultural and institutional divisions.[12]

II. Tongues and prophecy: tensions between Luke and Paul

Aimless public ecstasy of pneumatics with no thought of serving others caused Paul to sharpen the tension between tongues and prophecy and to prefer prophecy in the public assembly to uninterpreted tongues. For Paul, tongues are primarily for the secret discipline of private, unintelligible prayer, in which one speaks 'mysteries to God, not to people' (14.2), edifies the self (14.4) and praises God with the spirit, not with the understanding, thereby giving thanks (14.14–17). In this context, Paul seems to be a tongues enthusiast, even thanking God that he prays in tongues more than all of the Corinthians (14.18). But in the church, Paul prefers intelligible prophecy, allowing tongues only if they are interpreted (14.19, 27–28). In contrast to Luke, any reference by Paul to the public sign-value of tongues is negative, as a sign of judgment (14.20–25) or as unutterable groans in weakness for the redemption to come (Rom. 8.26), as we see in a mirror dimly (I Cor. 13.12).[13]

Though Paul contrasted public ecstasy with prophecy, early Israelite prophecy was quite ecstatic (I Sam. 10.9–11). But in the Old Testament there was also a resistance to the view that ecstasy can magically induce divine action (I Kings 18.25–29). Prophecy flowed instead from a keen insight into truth, including that which was socially and politically relevant (e.g., Amos 5.21–24); this was also the case in the New Testament, for Jesus promised prophetic inspiration for those who bear witness before kings and governors (Luke 21.12–15). Though keen in insight, the prophets were more or less caught up in some sort of ecstasy in response to the prophetic call and the urgency of the moment.[14] This sense of prophetic urgency is revealed in Jesus, who associated prophetic insight with the inauguration of the kingdom of God in history, particularly through the work of the Spirit to liberate and to heal those bound by sickness and oppression.

The kingdom announced in prophetic utterance is apocalyptic in the sense that it is not directed from this world but from God. Yet, contrary to apocalypticism, the prophetic word of the kingdom opens humanity to free and responsible participation in redemptive history.[15] Pentecostals view prophecy almost exclusively as spontaneous admonition and comfort among believers (I Cor. 14.3). What is lacking is a broader view of prophecy that would include more reasoned proclamation and social criticism.

The contrast of tongues and prophecy in Paul is not assumed by Luke, who is willing, at least in Acts 2, to grant tongues prophetic significance (Acts 2.18). Yet, tongues are not related merely to prophetic communication in Acts. Tongues are also associated with praise (2.26; 10.46), and Luke's accent in Acts 2 is as much on those who could not understand the meaning of the tongues of fire as on those who could. Nowhere outside Acts 2 do tongues communicate any content.[16] Many detect an older source in Acts 2 involving ecstatic tongues that was shaped by Luke into a prophetic event meant to symbolize the universal impact of the Gospel[17] and, perhaps, to respond to Paul's criticism of uninterpreted public tongues by placing the burden of responsibility on the hearers to be receptive and not on the speakers to interpret, in contrast to Paul (I Cor. 14.13–17). By way of contrast, one may argue that Acts 2 reflects an early blurring of the distinction between ecstatic tongues and prophecy, providing the background for the extreme devotion to ecstasy corrected by Paul.[18] It seems that a fluid relationship between unintelligible tongues and intelligible prophecy existed in the New Testament period.

Most importantly, Paul locates the public use of tongues in the context of a broad diversity of possible gifts, with no single gift claiming superiority over the other (I Cor. 12). Paul then places all gifts in relation to the love of Christ, which alone has ultimate significance for the people of God (I Cor. 13). All gifts, including tongues and prophecy, are to be judged by their effectiveness in confessing Jesus as Lord (12.3) and in building up the congregation in the love of Christ (13 and 14). Tongues must be submitted along with all other gifts to the standard of Christ and the scriptures.

III. The Pentecostal practice

Pentecostals commonly deal with the tensions between Luke and Paul on glossolalia by making functional distinctions between tongues as initial evidence (better: 'sign') (Luke) and tongues as a private prayer language and a congregational gift (Paul). Only the latter function is not potentially universal. Though this paradigm neatly categorizes the more fluid prophetic life reflected in the New Testament, it grants both Luke and Paul equal weight in a theology of tongues. The Pauline view of tongues does not cancel out Luke for Pentecostals, but sets limits on how Luke is to be interpreted.[19]

Tongues can be a *prodigium* in worship without gaining prominence over other gifts. Tongues can also have importance in both private self-edification and corporate witness.

Simon Tugwell noted that the essence of our humanity is hidden in the Word of God spoken at creation, and, we might add, in the incarnation of the Logos in Christ.[20] Prophecy is an effort to clarify that Word for guidance in confession and witness, but tongues symbolize the unfathomable depth of mystery still involved in this Word that is greater than us all. Tongues reveal the limits of the language of faith to penetrate this mystery, reminding us, in the words of Karl Barth, that all human language and culture are just temporary 'pilgrim's clothing' aiding us on our journey toward the discovery of our free humanity in Christ.[21] Whether one engages in tongues or prophecy, what is implied is the creative tension between the unspeakable mystery cried out from the depths and the urgency to speak a word that will glorify Christ and lead to faith, hope and love. In this tension, God lays claim to us in the depths and in our proclamation, or in the fount and in the spring that flows from it.

Notes

1. Compare Acts 2 with Philo's description of the voice of God at Sinai as a 'flame being endowed with articulate speech in a language familiar to the hearers', *The Works of Philo (Decalogue* 47), Peabody, Massachussetts 1993, 522. Many note a connection between Pentecost and Sinai as early as the first century, e.g., R. Pesch, *Die Apostelgeschichte* (1. Teilband), Evangelisch-Katholischer Kommentar zum Neuen Testament, ed. J. Blank et al., 101–2.

2. Jacques Ellul, *Prayer and Modern Man*, New York 1970, 10.

3. Kenneth Leech, *True Prayer*, London and New York 1980, 61–2.

4. William Samarin, *Tongues of Men and Angels*, New York 1972, 154, 232. An example of the many views on tongues can be gained from *Speaking in Tongues: A Guide to Research on Glossolalia*, ed. Watson Mills, Grand Rapids, Michigan 1986.

5. Paul Tillich, *The Protestant Era*, Chicago 1947, 94–112; F. D. Macchia, 'Tongues as a Sign: Towards a Sacramental Understanding of Pentecostal Experience', *Pneuma* 15.1, Spring 1993, 61–76. See also F. D. Macchia, 'Sighs too Deep for Words: Towards a Theology of Glossolalia', *Journal of Pentecostal Theology* 1, 1992, 47–73.

6. R. Baer, 'Quaker Silence, Catholic Liturgy, and Pentecostal Glossolalia: Some Functional Similarities', in *Perspectives on the New Pentecostalism*, ed. R. Spittler, Grand Rapids, Michigan 1976, 150–64.

7. W. Hollenweger, *Geist und Materie, Interkulturelle Theologie*, Vol. III, Munich 1988, 314–15; H. Cox, *Fire from Heaven. The Rise of Pentecostal Spirituality and the Reshaping of Religion in the Twenty-First Century*, Reading, Massachussetts 1995, 93.

8. Krister Stendahl, 'Tongues: The New Testament Evidence', in *The Charismatic Experience*, ed. M. P. Hamilton, Grand Rapids, Michigan 1975, 58.

9. M. Dempster, 'The Church's Moral Witness, A Study of Glossolalia in Luke's Theology of Acts', *Paraclete* 23.1, 1989, 1–7. According to H. Gunkel, tongues were the 'most striking characteristic activity' of the Spirit, *Influence of the Holy Spirit*, Philadelphia 1979, 25, 30, or, according to R. Pesch, the initial miracle of the Spirit's work, *Apostelgeschichte* (n. 1), 108. The Pentecostal doctrine of tongues as 'initial evidence' of Spirit baptism is not universally held among Pentecostals. It has provoked criticism recently as, for example, a wrongful search for 'proofs' of the Spirit's sovereign work: H. I. Lederle, 'Initial Evidence and the Charismatic Movement: An Ecumenical Appraisal', in *Initial Evidence*, ed. G. B. McGee, Peabody, Massachussetts 1991, 131–41. I have responded by suggesting the need for a doctrine of tongues as initial 'sign', shifting the focus from 'proofs' to sacramental encounter: 'Tongues as a Sign' (n. 5). C. M. Robeck notes that the Pentecostal founder William Seymour emphasized love and holiness over tongues as signs of the Spirit: 'William Seymour and the "Bible Evidence"', in *Initial Evidence*, ed. G. B. McGee, Peabody, Massachussetts 1991, 72–95.

10. J. Roloff, *Die Apostelgeschichte*, Das Neue Testament Deutsch V, Göttingen 1981, 45.

11. Russell Spittler, 'Glossolalia', *Dictionary of Pentecostal-Charismatic Movements*, ed. G. B. McGee et al., Grand Rapids, Michigan 1988, 441.

12. I am grateful to M. Volf for insight into the eschatological nature of catholicity: *Wir sind die Kirche*, Habilitationsschrift, Tübingen, 1993.

13. E. Käsemann notes that the groans are 'unutterable' in Romans 8.26, not 'unuttered', a paradoxical statement typical of responses to the eschatological Spirit. It makes more sense if the groans come from observable phenomena in worship: *Commentary on Romans*, Grand Rapids, Michigan 1980, 237–8, 241. See also Kasemann's 'The Cry for Liberty in the Worship of the Church', in *Perspectives on Paul*, Philadelphia 1971, 122–37. The Pauline reference to tongues of angels (I Cor. 13.1) may be another connection with the apocalyptic context of tongues, similar to the pseudepigraphical *Testament of Job*, 48–50, in which Job's daughters sing in tongues of angels. See, Spittler, 338.

14. G. von Rad, *The Message of the Prophets*, London 1968, 34.

15. The value of apocalypticism for theology is noted by W. Pannenberg, 'Constructive and Critical Functions of Christian Eschatology', *Harvard Theological Review*, April 1984, 123–7. The contrast of a prophetic to an apocalyptic orientation, however, is presented by M. Buber, 'Prophecy, Apocalyptic, and Historical Hour', in *On the Bible, Eighteen Studies*, ed. N. N. Glatzer, New York 1982, 172–87.

16. R. Gundry's association of tongues in the New Testament period merely with

miraculous proclamation in unlearned foreign languages is untenable: 'Ecstatic Utterance (NEB)?', *Journal of Theological Studies* 17, 1969, 299–307. This phenomenon, termed xenoglossia, is believed by many Pentecostals to have occurred in the modern era. Such a phenomenon, however, has not been scientifically verified.

17. Note, for example, G. Schneider, *Die Apostelgeschichte*, Herders Theologischer Kommentar zum Neuen Testament, ed. A. Wickenhauser et al., V. 1, Freiburg 1980, 243f.

18. The view of I. N. S. Engelsen, *Glossolalia and Other Forms of Inspired Speech According to I Corinthians 12–14*, PhD Dissertation, Yale University 1970, 147f.

19. On the hermeneutical principle involved in negotiating meaning between canonical witnesses from historically dissimilar traditions, G. T. Sheppard, 'Canonization: Hearing the Voice of the Same God in Historically Dissimilar Traditions', *Interpretation* 36, January 1982, 21–33.

20. Simon Tugwell, 'Speech-Giving Spirit, A Dialogue with Tongues', in *New Heaven and New Earth? An Encounter with Pentecostalism*, ed. S. Tugwell et al., Springfield, Illinois 1976, 136.

21. Barth, *Church Dogmatics*, eds. G. W. Bromiley and T. F. Torrance, Vol. III 4, Edinburgh 1961, 302.

Office and Spirit: A Catholic Response

Hermann Häring

This response to F. D. Macchia is concerned with a sore point in ecumenical dialogue. Since the 1970s, charismatic gifts have been valued highly in the Catholic Church:[1] even bishops and senior dignitaries have become involved in the charismatic renewal. Moreover the Pentecostal communities have become increasingly significant in the ecumenical context, to be taken seriously by all those who believe in the future of a reconciled Christianity.[2] But how can the Catholic Church find a place for the gifts of the Spirit, glossolalia and prophecy, in its hierarchical organization? May those who hold office in it pass judgment on the gifts of the Spirit, or does the last, virtually sacramental, word go to the charismatic word? I shall attempt to arrive at an answer in four stages.

I. Enthusiasm

No one can deny that the charisms grow out of natural preconditions. They derive from an intense religious experience and are embedded in certain patterns of behaviour. Granted, we encounter them on all continents, but it is no coincidence that the modern Pentecostal and charismatic movements did not come into being in Europe or in the bosom of Western culture. Certainly there has been an enthusiastic form of Christianity at all times,[3] but even in it charismatic gifts found only a limited echo. They were banished to the sphere of individual mystical experience, and today attract the interest of psychologists and sociologists, linguists and behavioural scientists. As Max Weber showed us, charismatic individuals can build up and stabilize structures of authority and power; so charisms and a church order are not in mutual contradiction.[4] We know of ecstasy, sighs and inarticulate cries in extreme situations; so these can happen outside Christian worship or religious events. Elsewhere, too, people can understand one another, even if their language breaks the rules of coded sounds and grammar. And finally, linguistics can tell us a good deal about the massive performative force of the word – articulated or inarticulate – and its power to form communities, through the interplay of word and answer or (as Karl Rahner demonstrated[5]) through the polarity of (ritual) action and sacramental word. Moreover liturgy, which is always concerned with the inexpressible presence of God, seems to love extraordinary statements and to go beyond the sphere of rationally ordered articulation. Moods and experiences are engendered; experience of unsuspected realities, values and expectations is intensified. What happens here transcends the framework of rational discourse and as a result strikes unaccustomed chords.

One need not be a Christian or a theologian to understand something else: in particular those who feel that they are living in an end-time can express themselves in this ecstatic way. The question of time is of crucial significance for understanding the early communities. There is talk of 'joy' in the Gospel of Luke (1.1) and in the Acts of the Apostles (2.46). We know how great the expectations had become, and to what a degree the fulfilment could already be experienced. According to Luke, the Spirit rests on Jesus (Luke 3.22; 4.18). Finally, it is poured out on the whole community (Acts 2). Hope has fulfilled itself here and now. If we take this confrontation with an unfulfilled present seriously, the charismatic gifts must be an ecumenical topic. They may not be banished into the sphere of special cases or simply be privatized, as they have been for a long time.

So are not glossolalia, prophecy and other charisms the expression of a specifically Christian truth or attitude? At first sight I do not notice any specific aspects in them, since amazement at the Immeasurable and the stunning experience of its presence can be found in many religions. Here, too, nature precedes grace – to cite a good theological rule. Paul seems to have recognized this, since according to him speaking in tongues is particularly significant for unbelievers (I Cor. 14.22). Unbelievers in particular are to fall on their faces in worship, because 'truly God is in you' (I Cor. 14.25). The biblical understanding and a Christian theological understanding have still to be established.

II. Endangered practice

Of course the charisms are gifts bestowed by the Spirit of God. But the important thing is for the extraordinary character of these phenomena to sharpen the senses for God's messianic future. However, by contrast with all 'natural interpretation', this conception gives inner impetus. From a biblical perspective the Spirit does not just come out of the blue; here we have no dervishes dancing in rapture. When the community, looking to the future, breaks bread 'with gladness of heart' (Acts 2.36), this joy stems from the hope of righteousness and a universal reconciliation. In the account of Pentecost, the tongues of the Spirit do not narrow the circle of those who understand, but overcome the babel of language. God's word transcends the limits of human speech. Here no overwhelming ecstasy comes about, but the impossible happens: all peoples find the way back to their original unity. Of course Catholic Christians are fond of pointing out that the apostles themselves become prototypes of the new possession of the Spirit. However, the miracle of speaking then pops up as a miracle of hearing, the success of which finally depends on the inner light of all those who believe and have themselves baptized. All people can belong: 'Jews and Greeks, slaves and free, men and women' (3.28).

But Macchia rightly points out that Paul is critical of the gifts of the Spirit.[6] He applies strict rules to the assessment of them. He watches zealously and concretely over the new thing that has come about: there are harsh controversies over the enthusiastic experiences. So he insists on the freedom of the children of God, which must be secured by critical dialogue with Israel (Gal. 3–5). As Paul now confronts the Jewish practice of his time with this new freedom, so he confronts the jubilant messianic expectation with the everyday life of the community and its lack of freedom, the splits in it, in which social and cultural conflicts break out afresh. At this point Paul's theology is very realistic, for in the apparently abundant power he also sees failure and spiritual weakness. He does not say, like Peter, 'God's Spirit has been poured out upon us, our daughters prophesy and the old relate their dreams,' but, 'For we do not know how to pray as we ought, but the Spirit himself intercedes with us' (Rom. 8.26). The old world, still imperfect, has us in its grip. This cosmos does not rejoice but sighs, and has still to wait for the revelation (Rom. 8.19).

This is undoubtedly the sound of the first disappointment. The trial of patience after the experiences of the resurrection creates a sober, critical tone. Just as in another context the Gospel of Luke calls for patience until the harvest (Luke 8.15), and II Peter points out that for the Lord 1,000 years are as a day (II Peter 3.8), so now the Spirit no longer appears as a revolutionary force which drives people forwards, but as an admonitory power which supports their weakness. The apocalyptic pangs have not been endured (Matt. 6.13). The ecstatic cry proves to be incomprehensible stammering. According to Ernst Käsemann,[7] this cry bears the whole burden of the cosmos, which sighs (with us). It bears the burden of humankind, which does not even know what kind of freedom has been promised to it.

Thus Paul confronts us with a paradoxical situation of understanding and incomprehension. Evidently we do not know ourselves well enough to be able to interpret our crying. Therefore the very person who emphasizes the ignorance of our prayer to the enthusiasts requires that all speaking in tongues must be understandable, a communicative element in worship. But is there an understanding of ignorance, a communication in the unspeakable and an actuality of what cannot be expressed? By what right does Paul subject speaking in tongues and 'sighing' to a further criterion?

The situation compels him to. The gifts of the Spirit have led to disturbances and splits in Corinth; enthusiasm is destroying the unity and creating apocalyptic chaos. So Paul feels that before people boast that they are near to salvation, they should become aware of their situation – otherwise all the enthusiasm will lead to disaster. This biblically inspired knowledge is directly topical.

III. The well-being of the community

The enthusiasts are not to blame for the disappointment. Perhaps they are just innocent of the world and naive. On close inspection, disappointment could already have been learned from the story of Jesus' life. In decisive moments, he too had endured the profane experiences of disappointment, of falling dumb, indeed of remoteness from God (Mark 15.14). The righteous man who was completely on the side of the godless was finally cursed on the cross (Gal. 3.13).

Paul draws the conclusions of this and warns against an enthusiasm which has a fatal effect because it imposes on the weak and the injured in a way which is unrealistic and lacks solidarity.[8] He reacts in a specifically Christian way by radically relativizing the gifts of the Spirit. He robs them of their sacramental matter-of-courseness and subjects them to a very human criterion.

For Paul, this criterion is community,[9] and so he puts translation above glossolalia. As Macchia shows well at the beginning of his article, the gift of interpretation is understanding as a kind of test or correction. For the cry which is not understood can serve as a means of communication only if it is a gift of the Spirit. In I Cor. 13 this criterion is described in an even more fundamental way as 'love'. This great hymn to love is therefore not to be understood as a romantic hymn. In an unyielding and matter-of-fact way Paul uses it to call for a solidarity which alone bestows Christian legitimacy on the enthusiasm of the Spirit. So how and in what conditions can charisms keep their place in the Catholic Church and be in harmony with the doctrinal claim of the magisterium?

IV. Ways of resolving the conflict: office and Spirit

Let's go back once again to Luke's concept of the church. There the church, under the leadership of the apostles, is enjoying a great pneumatic upsurge: there is no question that the understanding of office in the Catholic Church is clearly derived from this conception.

The apostles, and the bishops as their successors, understand themselves as the authentic bearers of the Spirit. Unfortunately the church fathers already develop a one-sided christological foundation for the authority of their office.[10] That has led to a serious narrowing of it, but discussing that problem does not get us any further. The question is, how can the Catholic Church find a place for the charismatic gifts in its hierarchical organization?

I have already indicated that even many Catholic clergy think it good that room should again be found for charismatic enthusiasm, if only as a protest against the intellectualization of many Christian forms of worship, especially within Western culture, which seems to have forgotten the Spirit.[11] Many have forgotten as a result of everyday liturgical practice that God is a mystery and that the Holy cannot be uttered. We have forgotten that this world with its blatant injustice brings us to the limits of rational communication, that sometimes only tears, cries or threats are appropriate. Moreover, the gift of the Spirit to believers has also never fully been denied, and in the great renewal of recent decades Catholic Christians have constantly claimed this right by virtue of their baptism.

Of course far-reaching differences remain. These include the matter-of-factness with which Pentecostal communities let charismatic events – from speaking with tongues to baptism in the Spirit – have their own dynamic. Here the burden of proof lies not with the charismatics but with their critics. By contrast, the Catholic Church places prior confidence, not in an extraordinary demonstration of the Spirit, which bears the burden of proof, but in apostolic continuity, i.e. the preservation of faith in a form which has been tested for centuries.

There is no intrinsic objection to either of these concepts. But what happens in times of crisis and disappointment? We should remember Paul. Charismatic gifts do not guarantee the truth in themselves, but must be subjected to the criterion of love.

Now this criterion can resolve many conflicts. Nevertheless, what contributes to the well-being of a community is not always clear. In this case must not further possibilities be found? Scripture offers three ways of resolving conflicts.

The first, the royal way, lies in controversy and arguments. Paul and later generations constantly canvassed their convictions and argued for them. The great splits in the church came into being when the power to do this became paralysed. From this perspective the charismatic vitality of a community can be regarded as indispensable; for it works as the exercise of public speaking (II Cor. 3.12). But this, too, offers no guarantee of a resolution of the conflict.

The second way is the gift of discernment; it too belongs in the classic canon of charisms (I Cor. 12.10; I Thess. 5.12). It can be understood as a gift of gifts, since it indicates of what spirit a form of behaviour or a statement is a child. This gift is of inestimable significance, because it states the decisive problem openly.[12] But even it offers no guarantee of the solution of the conflict.

There remains the third way, the classic description of which is in Matt. 18.15–20. In the end it is for the community to discern the spirits: 'What you bind on earth will be bound in heaven' (Matt. 18.18). It is within this framework that the right of the bishops and the pope to bind and lose (Matt. 16.18) has its justification.

But the reality of institutions is more complicated.[13] It is necessary always to begin with the first way, and this must always remain open. Those who depart from it put themselves in the wrong. The second way must also always be taken note of. It seeks spiritual depth and investigates the limits, the prejudices and the secret interests of our arguments.[14] Finally, the third way is the way of the great exceptions and is only to be taken in such cases. But above all, no office will function unless it, too, exposes itself to argument and the discernment of spirits.[15] Though it may claim this gift for itself in a special way, it must never fall victim to the illusion that it has sole possession of it.

This response has been written from a comparative perspective within the church. So the really critical point has not been discussed.[16] Paul asks very soberly whether the gifts of the Spirit are of use to the community. This includes the question whether and how today the gifts of the Spirit are orientated on a messianic future. Does charismatic spirituality nourish itself on particular themes or on the great charismatic word which excludes cultural, social and sexual differences? Only if the latter is the case is any further discussion superfluous. Charismatic discourse is topical only when it helps towards seeking, grasping and articulating a more redeemed future. But when that happens, it is also important in the Catholic Church as what more than twenty years ago Ernst Käsemann called 'the cry for liberty in the worship of the church'.

Translated by John Bowden

Notes

1. For its reception in Catholic-speaking Germany see H. Mühlen, *Einübung in die christliche Grunderfahrung* (2 vols.), Mainz 1976/1982.

2. K. McDonnell, *Presence, Power, Praise* (3 vols.), Collegeville, Minn. 1980; J. R. William, *The Era of the Spirit*, Plainfield 1971; id., *The Pentecostal Reality*, Plainfield 1972; P. Hocken, 'Charismatic Movement', in *Dictionary of Pentecostal and Charismatic Movements*, 1988, 130–60; id., The Pentecostal-Charismatic Movement as Revival and Renewal', *Pneuma, The Journal of the Society for Pentecostal Studies* 3, 1983, 31–47.

3. It is still worth reading R. A. Knox, *Enthusiasm. A Chapter in the History of Religion*, Oxford 1950; W. J. Hollenweger, *The Pentecostals*, Vol. 1, Peabody, Mass. 1988.

4. M. Weber, 'Die drei reinen Typen der legitimen Herrschaft', in *Gesammelte Aufsätze zur Wissenschaftslehre*, Tübingen ³1948, 478–88.

5. Karl Rahner, 'Priest and Poet', *Theological Investigations* 3, London and New York 1967, 294–317.

6. U. Brockhaus, *Charisma und Amt. Die paulinische Charismenlehre auf dem Hintergrund der frühchristlichen Gemeindefunktionen*, Wuppertal 1972.

7. E. Käsemann, 'The Cry for Liberty in the Worship of the Church', in *Perspectives on Paul*, London and Philadelphia 1969, 122–37.

8. For the theological context of the Pauline doctrine of charisms see E. Käsemann, 'Ministry and Community in the New Testament', in *Essays on New Testment Themes*, London 1964, 63–94.

9. H. Küng, *The Church*, London and New York 1968, 215–30, offers a systematic ecclesiological treatment which is important for Catholic theology.

10. H. Häring, 'Der Geist als Legitimationsinstanz des Amtes', *Concilium* 16, 1980, 534–9.

11. J. Suenens, *A New Pentecost?*, London and New York 1977.

12. J. D. G. Dunn, 'Discernment of Spirits – A Neglected Gift', in W. Harrington, *The Witness of the Spirit*, Manchester 1979, 79–96.

13. T. Rendtorff (ed.), *Charisma und Institution*, Gütersloh 1985.

14. G. Hasenhüttl, *Charisma. Ordnungsprinzip der Kirche*, Freiburg 1969.

15. K. Rahner, *Das Dynamische in der Kirche*, Freiburg 1958.

16. J. Moltmann, *The Church in the Power of the Spirit. A Contribution to Messianic Eschatology*, London and New York 1977, 300ff.

Word and Spirit – Spirit and Word: A Protestant Response

Michael Welker

'Therefore it (the Word of God) is a word of power and grace: when it meets the ears it gives the spirit within . . . The word, I say, and the word alone is the vehicle of the grace of God . . . It is a sure saying that the Spirit is received by faith through preaching (*ex auditu fidei*).'[1]

These statements of Luther's about Gal. 3.2f. are the model of a 'typically Protestant' priority of the Word over the Spirit. Right up to Frank Macchia's article, the objection has been made to this priority that it does not take the poverty and helplessness of the Word seriously. Those who give the Word priority over the Spirit simply do not see the inability of the Word to correspond to the riches and the mystery of the Deity. Nor does the priority of the Word over the Spirit do justice to the power of the Spirit. It is the Spirit which first enables people to speak from and to God. Where the word fails, with 'sighs that cannot be uttered' (8.26), the Spirit represents before God those who do not know how they are to invoke the deity and why they should ask for their salvation. Aren't these objections decisive?

I. The helpless human word – and the power of the Spirit

In a variety of ways, the Spirit of God must in fact keep 'helping our weakness'. Without the Spirit, human beings do not get religious insight and far-sightedness. Without the Spirit of God they do not get the power of faith and the language of faith. They remain uncertain how they are to call on God. Can they know God and the reality which God intends at all? The Spirit brings liberation from this uncertainty. The Spirit overcomes our uncertainty as to whether we can speak appropriately of God and God's salvation. The Spirit penetrates the 'inaccessible light' in which God dwells. The Spirit fathoms the 'depths of the Godhead'. From the knowledge of God we human beings can then perceive the true destiny of our reality and help others to share in this perception. However, the Spirit is not a quite simple power of orientation, a simple pointer towards what is constantly being sought. The Holy Spirit gives many gifts which by working together make testimony, proclamation, knowledge, liturgical celebration and spirituality possible. There are many gifts which we need not only for spiritual life but also for constructing an ethos which furthers life and cultivating it, and for 'service of God in the everyday world'.

The Spirit must do more than liberate us from our uncertainties in our religious orientation. It must also tear us away from false or deceptive religious, ideological and moral certainty. The one-sidednesses and the distortions of our perception of God and our talk of God and to God are put in question and overcome by the 'outpouring of the Spirit'. Because of our uncertainty *and* our false certainty, each time differing gifts of the Spirit have to correct and supplement our own gifts. The Spirit is poured out to strengthen our creativity and make creative criticism of our knowledge of God and our practice of faith possible. That means that we are built up and challenged 'from all sides' by the working of the Spirit.

The prophet Joel says that 'men and women, old and young, menservants and maidservants' all give prophetic expression to the knowledge of God when the Spirit is poured out (Joel. 3.1ff.). In the account of Pentecost (Acts 2.1ff.) we read that people of different languages, origins and cultural backgrounds together understand the talk of the 'mighty acts of God'. The 'body of Christ', built up by the Spirit, is similarly pluriform and has many members, rich in contrasts and fruitful differences. When Paul evokes 'unity in Christ' and unity in the Spirit, he never envisages an abstract and homogenous unity and equality, but the creative and living differentiated unity of the body with its different members (cf. I Cor. 12).

The outpouring of the Spirit is an event which works against all that is monochrome and one-sided, against all human claims to monopoly, all hierarchies that are of purely human origin and all shutting off of the self. The outpouring of the Spirit which comes to the aid of human weakness from all sides but which also breaks up false self-certainty and false religious certainties makes the helplessness of the human word unmistakably clear. Frank Macchia is quite right: here there is more than cognitive understanding. Here events and insights are realized which human beings cannot put into words. 'The tyranny of words' and the 'helplessness of words' are equally overcome. Not only thinking, hearing and speaking, but all human senses and capacities are claimed by the Spirit. No single gift of the Spirit may be a monopoly or claim a one-sided superiority for itself.

If the Spirit is allowed to work and is not massively hindered, if it is not 'driven away' (Wisdom 1.5), 'quenched' (I Thess. 5.19) or 'troubled' (Eph. 4.30), the community is built up richly. Certainly the human word has great importance and significance in it. But there can be no question of a priority of this word over the Spirit, whether in time or in hierarchy.

Now when he decisively gave priority to the Word over the Spirit, Luther did not have in view the human word which is sometimes helpless, sometimes selfish and high-handed, but rather the Word of God. As soon as this is clearly recognized, the question of priority and superiority must be put again.

II. The creative word of God – and the service of the Spirit in testimony

– 'Jesus Christ is the one Word of God' was the confession of the Barmen Theological Declaration in an utterly corrupt society and church.
– The Holy Spirit is the Word of God – by which we have to keep measuring our traditions, norms and convictions afresh. Thus the Reformation sparked off a theological controversy which for many people was only settled in principle by the Second Vatican Council.
– 'Law and gospel' are the two forms of the Word of God. To the present day there is reflection and puzzlement in systematic theology about the right way to distinguish between and relate these two forms.
– The word of God comes about in a threefold form: as revelation, scripture and preaching. How is this differentiation to be related to the

distinction between 'law and gospel'? How are the two differentiations connected with the christological determination of the word of God?

It is certainly not rash to say that we have very great difficulties in bringing the various basic statements and formulae of the high theologies about the 'Word of God' since the Reformation into a consistent relationship. And if we cannot achieve any clarity in understanding the 'Word of God', it is hardly surprising that the word should keep being understood only in the small area of human appropriation and attempts at appropriating the Word of God. The creative word of God, the Word which goes out, which can come to men and women for salvation and damnation, the Word by which creatures live, the 'imperishable seed', the 'source of all wisdom', the 'sword of the Spirit', then remains numinous.

A successful but deceptive theological simplification has made understanding the Word of God in our cultures considerably more difficult. This powerful but deceptive simplification claims that God's word always occurs in 'address'. The word of God occurs essentially 'in address' in a situation of dialogue, in the relationship between 'I and Thou', in the form of an encounter. That absolutizes a quite important aspect and the form of the Word of God and its activity, whereas it is only one aspect and form of the Word of God among other important aspects and forms.

This dialogical form results in a misunderstanding and distortion of the fact that the Word of God is not only effective in preaching that is perceived directly, but also surrounds us 'on all sides'. The 'abiding' of the Word of God in its many elaborations has thus become difficult to understand and easy to suppress. There has been a failure to recognize that the Word of God also supports us, challenges us and puts us in question where we do not want to perceive it or cannot perceive it directly. There is a failure to understand that the Word of God can come not only upon us dramatically, like a squall of rain, as Luther put it, but that it also works latently, in silence and in gently 'emergent' conviction. There has been a failure to recognize that the Word of God is also alive through persistent activity in what is hidden in each of us.

'Blessed is the man whose delight is in the law of God, who meditates on his law day and night,' says Psalm 1. 'But Mary kept all these words (words of the shepherds, words of the angel, words of God) and pondered them in her heart', says Luke 2. Certainly very few people in our Western cultures reflect day and night on God's law as it is written in the Old Testament. Presumably most people have considerable difficulty in getting a clear idea of what it means to 'ponder God's word in one's heart'. But at the same time our culture, our ethos, our morals and our forms of life, down to the rhythms of the weeks and the year, are deeply permeated and shaped by

God's Word. We may or may not want this or value it. We may caricature it, pervert it, suppress it, lament it or even fight against it. We may refer with the utmost justification to numerous distortions, improper appropriations and secularizations, good and bad. The effective power and traces of God's Word and the way in which it is appropriated by human beings are indisputably there in the deepest levels of our culture, or education; they have entered our norms and our visions great and small – in good things and in bad. But that means that the living and abiding word of God works on and through our forms of life and our norms. As a dynamic force it is at work in the depths of our societies and in our dispositions.

If we become aware of this power and force of the Word of God, this Word of truth, this Word which remains for eternity, this Word which supports us and comes over us, it becomes impossible to play off the 'power of the Spirit' against the 'helplessness of the Word'. Attributing the wonderful and the mysterious, what Frank Macchia calls the 'dramatic', only to the Spirit and the workings of the Spirit become questionable. The Word of God which edifies people, comforts them, raises them up, enlivens them, delights them, strengthens them, liberates them, allows them to hope, give them orientation and certainty; the Word of God which also puts them in question, terrifies them, binds them, oppress them, admonishes and judges them – this Word now seems to become virtually interchangeable with the Spirit of God in the fullness of its mystery and its drama. How can we play off the direct presence of Christ among a third of people living today and his indirect presence far beyond that; how can we play off the workings of the biblical traditions in a cultural history which goes back over millennia; how can we play off the power of the direct preaching in millions of communities on this earth every day and every week, and the many indirect emanations of this event, against the working of the Spirit?[2] How can we underestimate what is the certainly ambiguous, but equally certainly breathtaking and overwhelming power of the indirect activity of the 'word of God' in the most varied human appropriations?

Once we have even a remote idea of these dimensions of the Word of God – over and above its 'dialogical presence' in any form of address – we can understand why the biblical traditions speak of the Spirit as a really 'selfless reciprocal interpenetration', of a *perichoresis of Spirit and Word, Word and Spirit*. On the other hand, the Spirit does not bear testimony to itself but to Jesus Christ. The Spirit constantly leads towards God's Word. The Spirit makes God's Word constantly come anew to God's creatures. The Spirit links people with Christ, the 'one Word of God'. The Spirit binds, enlightens and clarifies the manifold testimonies of scripture in such a way that they point people to God and the reality intended by God.

Without the working of the Spirit, God's Word is fossilized in its use by creatures. It becomes rigid, loses its life and cannot be recognized as God's word. It can be abused and confused with the human word. But without the Word, the working of the Spirit cannot be distinguished from every possible demonstration of power and strength. It is the Word which distinguishes the Holy Spirit from all possible spirits, ghosts and demons. This word is a 'vehicle of the grace of God' because it first of all makes clear to creatures the working of the Spirit. The Word brings the power of God to create and create anew so near that human beings can accept and value it. Without the Spirit, human beings would be delivered over to their impotence and their false self-security. They would not recognize God's Word as a creative word of power which seeks to work on them and through them. But without the Word, human beings would be delivered over to the supremacy of the divine activity and the ungodly powers without the capacity for knowledge or the art of distinguishing. Only by being bound up in perichoresis with the Word does the Spirit of God show itself to be the Spirit of truth, of righteousness, of love and of peace.

III. Speaking with tongues – a 'mess of pottage' not to be despised

If we recognize the unity of Word and Spirit, Spirit and Word in perichoresis and their creatively changing relationships, we gain a clear perspective on speaking with tongues and the plain attitude of the biblical traditions towards it. The only central point in Frank Macchia's article to which I could not really assent was his repeated assertion that Paul and Luke are in tension over speaking with tongues. I cannot agree with him here. If we attempt to read the biblical texts without negative prejudice against speaking with tongues but also without a 'preferential option of tongues', instead we can get an amazingly clear picture.

It is not only Paul who quite clearly and unequivocally puts speaking with tongues below and after the prophetic gifts and other gifts of the Spirit.[3] The Acts of the Apostles also clearly distinguishes glossolalia which needs interpretation from what happens in the Pentecostal event. The miracle of the Pentecostal outpouring of Spirit does not lie in a glossolalia which would be dependent on the further gift of interpretation. The miracle of the Pentecostal outpouring of the Spirit lies in an *improbable common understanding in the midst of linguistic, cultural and social difference.* The Pentecost event and the outpouring of the Spirit is not about a speaking in tongues which cannot be understood and needs interpretation, but rather about a quite improbably universal comprehension and comprehensibility. Without doing away with the different tongues, without the different cultural allegiances and historical shapings, a differentiated universal community is created or manifested. Where there are no natural presuppositions for successful understanding, people brought together by the Spirit, grasped by the Spirit or affected by the outpouring of the Spirit can together take in the talk of 'God's mighty acts'.[4]

The Pentecost story describes a xenolalia, a speaking in foreign languages, not a glossolalia which is intrinsically imcomprehensible, a glossolalia which needs interpretation. The suggestion occasionally made, that Luke has turned glossolalia into xenolalia, is not supported either by this text or by the other mentions of the outpouring of the Spirit in Acts.[5] The other texts of Acts which speak of the outpouring of the Spirit (e.g. Acts 4.31; 8.15ff.; 10.44ff.; 11.15ff.; 15.8.; 19.2ff.) either give no further details of the consequences of the outpouring of the Spirit or emphasize the preaching connected with it. In the only two passages in which glossolalia is explicitly mentioned as a consequence of the outpouring of the Spirit, at the same time it is emphasized that this begins with the praise of God which can be perceived by outsiders and with prophetic discourse (Acts 10.46; 19.6). On this basis it does not seem advisable to make a distinction in principle between Paul and Luke.[6]

The close connection between Word and Spirit, Spirit and Word, brings Christians into an intimate and at the same time dramatic and powerful proximity to God. Through Word and Spirit men and women become children and heirs of God. They gain the power to understand God and God's intentions with creation and enter into a living and clear relationship with God. Compared to the close connection between Spirit and Word, Word and Spirit which is revealed and given to Christians and which we should always attempt to understand and value better, speaking with tongues is only a 'mess of pottage'. It is rightly put after the other gifts of the Spirit or clear prophetic discourse by the biblical traditions which emphasize this gift of the Spirit and reflect on it.

If we calmly note this subordination and move beyond making glossolalia the centre of a conflict of Spirit against Word and Word against Spirit, it would be surprising if many Christian churches on this earth could not make friends with this gift of the Spirit. We can understand how such a gift of the Spirit which is relatively 'remote from the Word' is almost polemically contrasted by some churches with the monological proclamation of the world that is 'remote from the Spirit' in other churches. We can understand the attempts to regain the multiplicity, liveliness and provocative power of the gifts of the Spirit in liturgical life by a concentration on speaking in tongues. We can understand how glossolalia in particular can make tangibly clear both the poverty *and* the riches of those who are seized by the Spirit. Alternative forms and understandings of the church, of liturgical life; alternative understandings of human beings and existence in faith which are expressed in the concentration on this gift of the Spirit, become at least remotely recognizable.[7]

If we free ourselves from the false, indeed fatal, opposition of 'Spirit against Word', 'Word against Spirit', we will be able calmly to accept the different weightings in the relationship between Word and Spirit, Spirit and Word. These different weightings in the different churches in fact lead to very different forms of theology, liturgy, spirituality and practice. If these weightings and the forms of life and thought that they produce have a basis in the biblical traditions, they can only further one another. The differences between churches, theologies, styles of piety are then no longer material for conflict and the occasion for reciprocal demarcations but sources of creative mutual challenge and fruitfulness.

And what about the clear priority of Word to Spirit in the remark of Luther's I quoted at the beginning? With his very sharp phrase, 'The Word, I say, and the Word alone is the vehicle of the Grace of God', we should contrast, in Luther's distinctive style: 'No, friend, where you make the Word out to be an active Word you must also make out the Spirit for me.' Despite all his notorious proneness to conflict and polemic, in this case the great controversialist would probably only have said 'Amen'.

Translated by John Bowden

Notes

1. M. Luther, *Kleiner Galaterkommentar*, 1519, WA II, 509.

2. For this see J. Moltmann's reflections on the relationship between the church as a fellowship of the invocation of the Spirit and the church as '*creatura verbi*' in *The Spirit of Life. A Universal Affirmation*, London and Minneapolis 1992, 230ff.

3. Cf. T. W. Gillespie, *The First Theologians. A Study in Early Christian Prophecy*, Grand Rapids 1994, 129ff. ('Prophecy and Tongues').

4. For a detailed discussion see M. Welker, *God the Spirit*, Philadelphia 1994.

5. For the deeper dimensions of linguistic competences beyond the alternative glossolalia – xenolalia ('language of the angels, etc'), cf. K. Berger, *Theologiegeschichte des Urchristentums. Theologie des Neuen Testaments*, Tübingen and Basel 1994, 367ff.

6. It needs to be explained why the clear reference to glossolalia is made only and precisely where Gentiles (Acts 10) and people who have not yet heard of the Holy Spirit (Acts 19) come to faith.

7. Whether we should accord speaking with tongues – like the sacrament – a prominent place in the 'proclamation of Christ's death until he comes' will similarly remain a matter for creative ecumenical dialogues and controversies, as will the notion that speaking with tongues could as it were represent a direct encounter with the 'eschatological Spirit', as Frank Macchia says.

Praying in the Spirit

A Pentecostal Perspective*

Steven J. Land

I. The impact of the Holy Spirit

Jesus Christ is the centre of the twentieth-century Pentecostal movement which has in one century circled the globe and influenced the entire Christian church. It has a depth and architectonic structure whose lineage can be traced through the nineteenth century Holiness Movement of the United States to John Wesley in eighteenth-century England, and through him to deeply ascetic, mystical, lay renewal and missionary movements, all the way back to the day of Pentecost.

Pentecostals confess Jesus Christ as saviour, sanctifier, healer, Spirit-baptizer and coming king. They testify that they have been saved, sanctified, healed and filled with the Spirit. This five-fold gospel of Jesus Christ and correlative testimony was the heart of the first ten years of the movement at the beginning of the twentieth century, and still characterizes it today. At its inception and in its majority expression, Pentecostalism affirms the cardinal doctrines of Christianity: the Trinity, the incarnation and atonement of Jesus Christ, the necessity of faith in Jesus Christ for salvation, the presence and power of God the Holy Spirit in every true believer, and the blessed hope of Christ returning to consummate the kingdom of God.

Pentecostalism has a distinctive ethos which may be characterized in terms of spirit-body correspondence, oral-narrative liturgy, fusion-fission tensions, and a crisis-development dialectic. Pentecostals are not gnostic, world-denying bodiless worshippers. They move together in praise, adoration, petition and intercession as the Spirit blows upon them. They practise anointing the sick and the laying on of hands for healing, dancing in the Spirit, offering the right hand of fellowship, embracing in familial bonds of love. Many practise footwashing as a sacrament of post-baptismal cleansing. They raise, hold and clap their hands in prayer and praise to God. The whole body is engaged by the Spirit in the worship of God.

Their liturgy is an oral-narrative display of fellowship as participation in praise, proclamation, witnessing, testimonies, and songs which narrate a journey into and with God, and, of course, there are prophecy, tongues and interpretation. The teaching and the preaching of the Word is central to their worship and witness. Their worship is a cathedral of sound.

Under the impact of the Holy Spirit, there are fusion-fission tensions which are indicative of the already-not yet character of the kingdom of God for which they fervently long. Because the kingdom is present through the Holy Spirit in the kingly reign of Jesus, faith and works are fused in love; fruit and gifts are fused in the holistic witness to the gospel which comes in word and demonstration and power of the Spirit. But some things are better characterized by fission. There is a sharp distinction between believers and unbelievers, church and world, God and Satan. There is a radical call to repentance, an invitation to come from darkness into light. There is also a radical call to holy living on the part of those who testify to being filled with the *Holy* Spirit in order to bear witness to the *Holy* Saviour.

The Christian life in this spirituality may further be characterized by a crisis-development dialectic in a manner analogous to that of the biblical drama in which the events of creation, the call of Abraham, the people of Israel, the coming of Jesus Christ, the outpouring of the Holy Spirit, etc., are seen as crises within and with a view toward a particular salvation-historical development. Thus Pentecostals speak of being saved, sanctified, filled with the Holy Spirit, healed, led to do certain things, etc. These crises or events of divine intervention are within and with a view towards the ongoing salvation-historical drama of redemption in which Pentecostals see themselves no longer as victims, but as participants in the missionary movement of God towards the consummation of the age in these last days.

Pentecostals are deeply grateful that God has delivered them from darkness into light. They are compassionately disposed towards the world and long for the salvation and healing of lost and hurting people because of the sanctifying grace of God. They are filled with courage and hope through being filled by the Holy Spirit, who enables them to speak in the eschatological language of the kingdom which is already, but not yet consummated. These essential Christian affections (fruits of the Spirit) of gratitude, compassion and courage correspond to the cardinal virtues of faith, love and hope, and are to be correlated with the righteousness, love and power of God which is their source.

II. Praying in the missionary fellowship

Pentecostal affections are shaped and expressed through the prayers of missionary fellowship. There the heart is formed for worship and witness as mutually conditioning aspects of Christian discipleship. The corporate and individual prayers are shaped by the preaching and teaching of the Word, the singing of songs, the giving and hearing of testimonies and prayer requests, the fellowship of believers before, during and after the services, the constant praises and thanks offered throughout the service, the operation of the various gifts of the Spirit, and the intercessions of the saints. All these activities shape the prayers, and the prayers in turn shape the affections. Pentecostalism is not emotionalism. These affections can only be understood in relation to their source and *telos* in God. They are what it means to be rightly related to God. They characterize the believers and become reasons for their practices of worship and witness. They are fundamentally Christian, and have a distinctively Pentecostal shape because of the distinctiveness of Pentecostal spirituality.

Prayer in the missionary fellowship is the primary means of participation in worship and is a rehearsal for witness. One remembers, acknowledges and anticipates the mighty acts and faithfulness of God in prayer. It is this memory and anticipation which evokes gratitude, informs compassion, and undergirds courage. Often the testimonies of the believer, usually offered in regular 'testimony services', will be in the form of a prayerful meditation on the individual's life which is then responded to by the community. These testimonies usually end with a request that the body will pray for certain needs, that the believer's life will be a blessing, and that he or she will finally 'make heaven their home'.

In seasons of 'concert prayer' it sounds as if the congregation is an orchestra warming up for the concert rather than playing the same musical arrangement. Sometimes the corporate prayers are like a jazz performance with first this and then that one improvising from a common theme; and at other times it is as if all are playing one great symphony of praise. There are praises, silences and periods of waiting on the sovereign Spirit. Sometimes the body will come together for hours to intercede for a special need. Or the church will go on an extended fast, thus accentuating the idea of prayer as 'waiting on the Lord'. Such waiting is essential for focus and affective transformation.

Prayer is the primary theological activity of Pentecostals. All worthwhile knowledge must be gained and retained prayerfully because only the Spirit can lead into all truth. Even correct knowledge will lead to presumption without constant praise, thanksgiving and intercession. A church that rejoices, waits and yields in the Spirit, a church that loves the Word and will tarry as long as it takes to pray through to the will of God, the mind of Christ and the leading of the Spirit – that church is Spirit-filled.

Prayer, therefore, is the most significant activity of the Pentecostal congregation. It suffuses every other activity and expresses the affective richness of the believer and the church. All prayer is in the Spirit, and all who truly pray continually open themselves to and receive what the Spirit is saying and doing in and among them. To receive and to be indwelt by the Spirit of Christ is to be a Christian. This indwelling and constant receptivity constitutes the church as a missionary fellowship or participation in God. All who have the indwelling witness of the Spirit to Jesus Christ are to be witnesses to him. Being a part of the missionary fellowship is being a part of the family of God. The church is God's home in which there are fathers and mothers in Zion and sisters and brothers in training for their fundamental Christian vocation: witness.

III. Being filled with the Spirit

Central to the Pentecostal practice of prayer is the view of fullness or filling with the Spirit. All Christians pray in the Spirit. But what do Pentecostals mean by Spirit-filled prayer? The possibility, some would say inevitability, of spiritual pride is a clear and present danger, because this would seem to imply a greater development of the fruit of the Spirit, and a greater openness to and desire for spiritual gifts. This subsequent experience of filling would seem of necessity to create two classes of Christians: the indwelt and the filled. Perhaps a brief discussion of filling or fullness will show how Pentecostals seek to avoid this danger.

The spiritual disciplines associated with the consecration are designed to give God more of the heart and to eliminate those things contrary to God's nature and will. To be filled was to be determined in a decisive way by the Spirit. This is analogous to the idea of being filled, for example, with fear. When this happens one will either flee or fight – or perhaps be totally immobilized. Fear fills the heart and orientates the entire person. Thus, to be filled with the Spirit is to be determined decisively by the things of the

Spirit, by what the Spirit is saying and doing. The fruit of the Spirit's indwelling is given a deeper intensity and, in the eschatological community of Pentecostalism, a new urgency.

To be filled with the Spirit and opened to greater fruitfulness has implications for the character and vocation of the believer. Others who claim no such filling or baptism of the Spirit may appear and actually be more stable personalities. Many have made more converts and many have greater Christian knowledge and insight. The first Pentecost, like those subsequently, took what the disciples were and set it on fire. They still had much to learn and to unlearn. There were still going to be differences of opinion, depression and struggles. But there is no denying the dynamic impact and charismatic character of the post-Pentecost community.

Pentecostals testify that they are stronger, more open, more useful than they used to be prior to baptism and being filled with the Holy Spirit. They continually seek the filling of the Spirit. For, though they speak of one Spirit baptism, they testify to repeated fillings. Saying that one wants to grow and that one wants to be filled with the Spirit may or may not be the same thing because Spirit baptism is fundamentally for the vocation of the believer as the witness in the power of the Holy Spirit.

When the Spirit comes to indwell the believer in regeneration, the Spirit brings the Son and the Father. The living of God in the believer and the believer in God – a mutual indwelling – makes the Christian, and the church as a whole, a habitation of God through the Spirit. Praying in the Spirit is intercourse or deep communion with God. It is to be 'on fire for God'. Being filled with the Spirit is being yielded to, directed and empowered by God to give a witness more consistent with God's Spirit to Jesus Christ. Sins against the Spirit hinder that witness, divide the missionary fellowship and distort the Christian affections.

Indeed a consideration of sin in relation to the Spirit adds a needed corrective to the one-sided view of sin as transgression with its resultant moralism. In Scripture the Holy Spirit may be resisted (Acts 7.51), grieved (Eph. 4.36), insulted (Heb. 10.29), quenched (I. Thess. 5.19), lied to (Acts 5.3,4) and blasphemed (Matt. 12.31; Luke 12.10; Mark 3.21, 29). To think of opposite kinds of responses would indicate something of what it would mean to be filled with the Spirit.

Every spirit from God will testify in word, deed, and character to the incarnate Son who had the Spirit without measure. The Spirit-filled community is the best safeguard against deception of the world, flesh or devil. The Scripture is the story of righteousness and truth. The Spirit creates hunger and thirst for righteousness and leads into all truth. Canon and charisma as given in the Spirit and received in the body of Christ are mutually conditioning. Neither can be explained or benefited from without the other. Ultimately, without the Scripture there is no path. Without the Spirit there is no light. The fruit of the Spirit is the character of God and therefore is depicted fully and narratively for believers in the life of Jesus. But the acts of Jesus must be taken together with the acts of the Spirit and the story of God the Father throughout Scripture, for all three of these are parts of the one story which should evoke and shape the Christian life for the kingdom of God. Prayer is the fundamental vocation of the community and each believer. It is the practice which shapes and evokes the affections, and is essential to discernment and every other gift. Out of the heart affected toward God, the Father, through God the Son and in God the Holy Spirit, the mouth speaks.

Pentecostal prayer is offered in three forms which shape and express the affections, each in its own way. These forms are: with words understood, without words, and with words not understood by others, but meaningful to the believer. I will now correlate each mode of prayer with a particular affection in order to illustrate the way in which these modes overlap and are mutually interpenetrating.

The first and most obvious mode of prayer is with words understood or prayer in the vernacular. Pentecostal prayers have been shaped primarily by the Bible and the understanding of the Christian life which has been mediated through the early Holiness Movement. Gratitude has been the most commonly expressed prayer of the Pentecostal congregation. Thanks for what God has done and praise for who God is are continually offered in Pentecostal worship. The presence of the Spirit is most characteristically responded to in this way.

But sighs, groans and laughter also express and shape the affections. Compassion motivates the intercessory prayers of Pentecostals as they weep over the lost and afflicted and long for the coming of the Lord. Prayer as sighs is evoked by the Spirit who groans as does all creation for the full and final manifestation of the sons and daughters of God. 'Holy laughter' is also common as believers experience the comfort and joy of the Spirit and meditate upon the eschatological promises and vision. Thanksgiving, love and confidence are indicative of the 'already' of what God has done, is doing and will do, whereas petitionary longing, rejoicing and praise because of the promised victory, and courageous waiting through hard trials, are more indicative of the 'not yet' quality of the affections.

Speaking in tongues, the most studied and discussed aspect of Pentecostal piety, is a form of prayer which is especially edifying to the individual; it gives assurance, confidence and courage. The end began in Jesus Christ and is coming to consummation. This speech creates and sustains a community whose culture is situated simultaneously in the 'already' and 'not yet' of eschatological existence. Not all will exercise this gift of tongues in the body; but for Pentecostals, all may speak in tongues in self-edification, which will, in the unity of the body, ultimately if indirectly edify the whole. Speaking in tongues as evidence of Spirit baptism is a Pentecostal doctrine which was developed to answer the early charges that Pentecostals were either deranged or demonized. Pentecostals agree with the apostle Peter, who testified that the tongues-speech in the house of Cornelius was evidence of Spirit baptism (Acts 10.46). Speaking in tongues is thus a sacrament of the eschatological Spirit who emboldens and empowers by giving voices of praise to the victims whom the world has told to shut up. Speaking in tongues may be seen in a manner analogous to the kiss offered in the covenant service of marriage. The kiss symbolizes and mediates the covenant bonds and celebrates the delight in one another. Speaking in tongues for the Pentecostal is not law; it is gospel. God has provided this means of edification to every believer, and places this gift in the church where, with interpretation, this is as blessed as prophecy.

All prayer, as noted earlier, is in the Spirit. The three modes suggest that the whole of the personality is to be engaged in prayerful dialogue and communion with God. Further, the threefold shape of prayer indicates that affections are not only complex, cognitive integrations but that they also operate on and are expressions of different levels or dimensions of human consciousness. This is true whether one's culture is oral-narrative or literate. First and Third World participants are in need of such searching, formative and multi-dimensional prayer. All three modes of prayer are interdependent and mutually conditioning. In prayer the Holy Spirit continually sanctifies believers so that the structure, content and dynamics of God's holiness are reproduced in Christians as righteousness, love and power. These three correspond to the gratitude, compassion and courage used earlier to characterize Pentecostals.

The modes of prayer are modelled and practised in the missionary fellowship as the fundamental means of forming and expressing the distinctive affections. The witness, fruit, gifts and filling with the Holy Spirit contribute to a single unifying passion which orders the affections and directs them to a single goal: the kingdom of God.

IV. A passion for the kingdom

The kingdom of God is God's rule or reign. It is that society and situation in which persons, created by God in the divine image, love God and their neighbour with their entire being. The kingdom is 'present and future', 'already and not yet', 'in but not of this world'. The community of Christ acknowledges and agrees to submit joyfully to this reign. The passion for the kingdom of God is the organizing principle, the integrative centre of the affections.

Praying for the kingdom of righteousness and walking in the light are ways of shaping and expressing the affection of gratitude. Giving thanks is a fundamental recognition that one's life and the kingdom are God's gift. Praise and gratitude mean living to the praise of God's glory and walking in the works ordained from the foundation of the world to glorify God and to seek the welfare of the neighbour.

Several times it has been noted that living in the presence of God is crucial to Christian spirituality and especially Pentecostal piety. This does not entail living with certain constant sensations, nor is it merely a mental exercise. There is a daily vital experience of placing one's self at the disposal of the Spirit as the source of and director of life (Gal. 5.25). The disciplines of private and corporate prayer, living in the Scriptures, walking in fellowship, the Lord's Supper, fasting and mortification, all are ways of learning to attend to the Spirit in following Christ. Living in the presence of God, walking in the light and delighting in the Lord are all aspects of the same thing. This is what it means to know God.

Being baptized in or filled with the Spirit is a way of speaking of the integration of these aspects of the Christian life. The joy of the Lord is a strength, encouragement and source of hope. This joy is the fruit of the Spirit who gives the believer a 'taste' of the power of the age to come. Sometimes even a taste will cause the believer almost to lose consciousness. The ecstasy of Pentecostals is not a possession or loss of self-control. It is a relinquishment of control in a trust that believes that salvation is a gift of God that has nothing to do with self-willed and technique-manipulated progress but has everything to do with the power of the God who raised Jesus and sends the Spirit with witness and wonders into the community of hope. This enjoyment is most often a quiet, constant, abiding sense of God's leading and providence. But it is also – and the two are mutually reinforcing – characterized by moments of unspeakable joy.

All gifts of the Spirit are eschatological, proleptic signs of a kingdom of joy where sorrow, death and sin are put down and will be banished once and for all. Speaking in tongues may express the painful longing of joy or its exultant victory, but true joy always instils courage to press on to the kingdom. Healings, of ailments from a headache to a heart attack, are provisional, temporary inducements to rejoice, because the Father is going to give the kingdom to the poor who seek first the kingdom and his righteousness. When it is kept in mind that most Pentecostals are poor, non-white, Third World, young adults, it is no wonder that this renewal in the Spirit, this anticipatory celebration of the kingdom, is so often characterized by laughing, leaping and praising God. The passion for the kingdom is the ruling affection of Pentecostal spirituality.

Note

* This article is taken largely, but with some modification, from Steven J. Land, *Pentecostal Spirituality: A Passion for the Kingdom*, Journal of Pentecostal Theology Supplement Series 1, Sheffield 1993.

Divine Liturgy and Jesus Prayer: An Orthodox Perspective

Constantine Fouskas

I. The liturgies in use

Of all the integral liturgies which are in use in the Orthodox Church today, the *Liturgy of Saint John Chrysostom* is the shortest and best known; it is celebrated most frequently and is most beloved by the congregation. It is celebrated throughout the year, on any day, and always in the mornings. This liturgy is not completely a work of Chrysostom, but it is an arrangement and completion by Chrysostom of the liturgy which was being celebrated at Antioch in his time. Ancient tradition does not identify this liturgy as Chrysostom's work, although it was well known that Chrysostom composed liturgical prayers.

The *Liturgy of Saint Basil the Great* is the most extensive, because the prayers contained in it are much more extensive than those in the Liturgy of Saint John Chrysostom. It is celebrated after the latter, always in the mornings, ten times a year.[1] The view that Basil reformed and extended a shorter liturgy which was already in existence can hardly be maintained today: Gregory the Theologian, Peter the Deacon, Leontius of Byzantium and others testify that Basil composed his own liturgy from the start, though of course he had in mind the liturgical texts extant in his day.

The *Liturgy of the Preconsecrated Gifts*[2] is not an integral liturgy, because the part relating to the consecration of the gifts, the anaphora, is omitted. This is why a more sacred host soaked with the consecrated wine, i.e. Christ's blood, from an integral liturgy celebrated on a Saturday or Sunday is kept in the monstrance. This liturgy differs from the Liturgies of Basil and Chrysostom in many other ways; in particular, it is associated with Vespers and has readings only from the Old Testament. Readings from the Gospels and the Apostles take place only when this liturgy is celebrated on the feast day of a 'celebrated saint'; when it is celebrated on the first three days of Holy Week there is only an apostolic reading. This liturgy is celebrated every Wednesday and Friday of Lent and on the feast days of a 'celebrated' or local saint, if these feasts coincide during Lent, and on the days Monday, Tuesday and Thursdays.

These three liturgies belong to the Byzantine liturgical type, even if they have been elaborated, or have similarities with other anaphoras or liturgical types.

The so-called *Liturgy of Saint James* (Antiochene type) is hardly ever celebrated in the Orthodox Church. Because it is so long, it is usually celebrated on 12 October and 26 December, feasts of St James. The so-called *Liturgy of Saint Mark* (Alexandrian type) has been displaced by the Byzantine liturgy; it is not celebrated today even in the area of the Orthodox Patriarchate of Alexandria, and is almost unknown. At most it is celebrated for the practice of divinity students after special permission from the ecclesiastical authorities. The so-called *Anaphora of Clement*, a text from the fourth century, which in ancient times was considered to be an authentic text of Clement of Rome for liturgical use, is now completely ignored and treated by specialists as a text of Pseudo-Clement.[3]

II. The christological dimension

The following aspects of the christological dimension of the liturgies of the Byzantine type are to be noted.

During the Small Entrance of the liturgy, which symbolizes Christ's appearance in public and his acts, the Third Antiphon is sung. This is a well-known hymn which runs: 'Only-begotten Son and Logos of God, who being immortal yet didst condescend for our salvation to be incarnate through the Most Holy Theotokos and Ever-Virgin Mary and without change didst become man; Who was crucified, subduing death by death,

Christ our God, who art one of the Holy Trinity, glorified with the Father and the Holy Spirit, save us.'[4] Despite its brevity, this hymn contains in brief a great deal of christological teaching. Through the hymn this teaching comes to the congregation, which is better able to understand dogmas than to formulate them.

Saint Chrysostom, commenting on Christ's incarnation, says: 'He who surpasses every mind and conquers every thought, who has gone before angels, archangels and every spiritual power that exists above, condescended to be a man and to take flesh made of earth and mud, and to be conceived in a virgin's womb, there to stay for a nine-month period, and to feed on milk and suffer every human thing.'[5]

In the prayer which comes before the Cherubic Hymn there is a formulation with a special christological meaning: 'For thou art he who offers and he who is offered, he who receives and he who is received and distributed.' Here, Christ is presented as a sacrificing high priest, as a victim, as one who receives sacrifice and as everlasting food for believers. This christological formulation of the Liturgies of St Basil and St Chrysostom, nowadays attributed to St Cyril of Alexandria,[6] is an excellent one. Epiphanius of Salamis, writing against the Melchizedekians, says that Christ the Lord, pre-existing as 'Holy God-Logos from God, the Son of God who was born without authority and time', was born as a man.[7] Then Christ offers his priesthood to the Father, according to the order of Melchizedek. 'He, being victim, offering, sheep, lamb, everything for us, so that he would come for us as real life, and his priesthood might become the immovable support.'[8]

At the most sacred point in the celebration of the eucharist there is a reference to the central events of Christ's offering and sacrifice, i.e. his crucifixion, burial and resurrection, in the following christological prayer: 'Remembering this saving commandment and all that has been done for us, the cross, the grave, the resurrection on the third day, the ascension into heaven, the enthronement at the right hand and thy glorious second coming, we offer to thee thine own from thine own, in all and for all.' It is characteristic that hymns and prayers in the liturgy are composed in the plural. This has great theological significance. As G. Florovsky writes: 'This unity, which surpasses the divisions of time, is revealed and shown already in the liturgical experience of the church, especially in the eucharist. There is not only the local community of living believers gathered before the holy altar; rather, the whole Catholic Church is really present whenever the sacred mystery of unity is celebrated. Because Christ is never separated from his body.'[9] After this prayer comes the consecration of the holy gifts, which is difficult to express in human words. That is why Chrysostom commends silence and devotion to us: 'Then revere that altar from which all of us receive Christ who was sacrificed for us and who is the victim laid on it.'[10]

III. The function of Jesus prayers

The holy liturgy and the introduction to its rites contain many prayers addressed to Jesus Christ. It is impossible to even mention them all here, so just a few will be quoted briefly.

In the regular night prayers we read: 'Christ our God, who every time and hour is worshipped and glorified in heaven and earth'; here we ask Christ to hear our prayer and to help us to keep his commandments in our life. At this time and at many other times we recite a deeply spiritual prayer, 'Lord and ruler of my life', which is attributed to Saint Ephraem.

In the hours of prayer there is the superb prayer to Christ: 'Christ, who art the true light which lights and sanctifies every one who comes into the world, let the light of your person come to us so that we may see the invisible light. And direct our steps to practise your commandments, through the intercession of your all-holy Mother and all the Saints, Amen.'[11]

In the short rite of *Kairos*, a prayer inserted into Matins, in which the priest asks mercy from the Lord and 'permission' to celebrate the liturgy, there are four special prayers. The last one is as follows: 'Stretch forth thy hand, Lord, from the height of thine holy dwelling and strengthen me to conduct thy service, so that, standing uncondemned before thine awesome altar, I may offer the bloodless sacrifice; for thine is the power and the glory, now and for ever, Amen.'

While the priest is putting on his vestments he says six prayers to Christ, the content of which is doxological and dithyrambic. The first is: 'My soul will rejoice in the Lord, for he has clothed me with the cloak of salvation and with the robe of delight; he has crowned me with a mitre as a bridegroom and adorned me as a bride, now and for ever, Amen.'

The first part of the text which the priest utters when cleansing his hands before the preparation of the Holy Gifts is a prayer to the Lord which is called the vow of *Proskomide*: 'I cleanse my hands with innocence, Lord, and so I will approach thine altar; that I may hear the voice of thy praise and tell of thy wonderful deeds to all men. Lord, I have loved the habitation of thine house, and the place where thine honour dwells.'

Besides the prayers to Christ already mentioned, the following prayers in the liturgy deserve to be cited.

Prayer of the Readings: 'Lighten our hearts, merciful Lord, with the pure light of thy knowledge, and open the eyes of our minds to perceive thine evangelical teaching . . . '

Prayer of the Cherubic Hymn: 'None of those who is entangled in carnal desires and pleasures is worthy to approach and serve thee, the King of glory . . . Thee I approach, and to thee I bow my head and pray: Turn not thy face from me nor reject me from among thy children, but deem me worthy to offer thee these gifts. For thou art he who offers and he who is offered, he who receives and he who is received and distributed, Christ our God . . . '

Prayer before reciting the Lord's Prayer: 'Unto thee, merciful Lord, we entrust all our life and hope and we beseech and pray and supplicate thee, Deem us worthy to receive thy heavenly and awesome mysteries that are upon this holy and spiritual table with pure conscience for the remission of sins, the forgiveness of transgressions, the communion of the Holy Spirit, the inheritance of the kingdom of heaven and freedom to come near Thee, not for judgment or condemnation.'

Prayer before breaking the bread: 'Hear us Lord Jesus Christ our God, from thy holy dwelling-place and from the throne of thy kingdom; thou who art with the Father above and existing[12] with us unseen, come and sanctify us and by thy mighty hand impart to us thy sacred body and precious blood, and through us to all peoples.'

Before the taking of Holy Communion there are six superb prayers referring to the priest's and people's participation. Between these prayers come the verses:

Behold, I draw near to Holy Communion,
O Creator, do not burn me as I partake of it,
for thou art a fire that consumes the unworthy;
cleanse me therefore from every stain.

After the taking of Holy Communion the priest recites this prayer for all the congregation: 'We thank thee, Lord and lover of humankind and benefactor of our souls, that thou hast deemed us worthy today to partake of thy heavenly and immortal mysteries. Direct our ways; establish in us thy fear, watch over our life, strengthen our endeavours; through the intercession of the Theotokos and Ever-Virgin Mary and all the Saints. Amen.'

It is true that in every rite of the Orthodox Church there are prayers to Christ, the content of which is glorifying and merciful. Those who want to investigate them must research the subject fully, without limitations. However, in this short article explaining what prayers there are in the rite in general and the Holy Liturgy in particular, and of what kind they are, it is possible only to make a selection. For the non-Orthodox those mentioned may already seem too much, but to Orthodox theologians the treatment will have seemed all too short.

Notes

1. On the five Sundays of the Great Lent, on Thursday and Saturday of Holy week, on the eves of Christmas and Epiphany and on the Feast Day of St Basil.

2. The author of this liturgy is unknown. Among those suggested is Gregory the Great, the so-called Dialogos, and this opinion has been accepted by many specialists. Cf. N. Zemov, *The Christian East*, London 1956, 51.

3. *Constitutiones Apostolorum through Clement*, VIII, 12, 35–9. See my *Nicholas of Methone and His Teaching on the Holy Eucharist*, Athens 1992 and 1995, 135–9 (in Greek), for this twelfth-century figure.

4. The translation of this passage and some others from the liturgy come from Archbishop Athenagoras, *The Liturgy of the Orthodox Church*, London 1979.

5. 'On the "Father, if it is possible"', para. 3, Migne, *Patrologia Graeca* §1, 37.

6. See John Meyendorff, *Byzantine Theology*, New York 1983, 40.

7. *Against Heresy* II, 1, 35, Migne, *Patrologia Graeca* 41, 980c.

8. The theologian Nicholas of Methone in three of his works comments on the eucharist and in particular on the phrase 'You are the one who offers'. See my *Nicholas of Methone* (n. 3), 124–48.

9. G. Florovsky, *The Body of the Living Christ. An Orthodox Interpretation of the Church*, Thessaloniki 1972, 48 (in Greek).

10. 'On Romans 8.8', Migne, *Patrologia Graeca* 60, 465.

11. This prayer is repeated many times in many rites.

12. All celebration in the liturgy is done in the name of the Holy Trinity and especially in the name of Jesus Christ, who is not only present but does as the great high priest whatever the human celebrant is unable to do. This is expressed wonderfully by Chrysostom (*On Matthew*, 82, 5, Migne, *Patrologia Graeca* 58, 744): 'What is celebrated here is not a work of human power. The one who did this at that supper is also doing it now. We (= the priests) are servants, but he who sanctifies and changes the gifts is Christ. This altar is that Table and is not diminished. Because Christ does not create only that one, but this one too.'

In Spirit, Mind and Body: A Catholic Reponse

David N. Power

In responding to the paper by Steven Land, I have been invited by the editors of this issue of *Concilium* to address my comments chiefly to the question of worship. Areas of convergence and agreement in this matter between Pentecostals and Roman Catholics have been noted in various meetings between designated Roman Catholics and members of Pentecostal groups.[1] I shall address it under three headings, inspired by Land's paper, seeking to search out the areas of convergence, even within divergence, between Catholic practice and Pentecostal practice. These headings are: (*a*) worship in the Spirit; (*b*) body and worship; (*c*) worship and kingdom.

I. Worship and Spirit

The history of Catholic liturgy has not been strong in its invocation of the Spirit, and Catholic sacramental theology before the mid-point of this century gave little attention to the action of the Spirit in prayer and worship. If a change has come about in this matter, it is largely due to greater exchange with Eastern and Orthodox traditions. Of late, interaction with Pentecostals, on both a formal and practical basis, has in turn opened up new perspectives on the action of the Spirit in prayer. Most important of all for Catholic liturgy is the understanding that all that is done in worship is done in the power and with the gifts of the Holy Spirit, shaping both our remembrance and acclamation of Christ, and our turning to God from present need. Under these influences, what is most readily picked up by Catholic communities from the Western tradition is the teaching of Saint Augustine on unity in charity and in the Spirit. Though he accepted the validity of baptism given outside the communion of the one faith, he thought that it brought no grace unless celebrated in the unity of the Spirit and of love. This community is for Catholics the greatest sign of the gift of the Holy Spirit and the greatest witness to the Lordship of Jesus Christ.

Within the action of this community, however, there is the contribution of many gifts and many ministries from within the body of the church. In looking back to New Testament foundations of communal worship, Catholics have gone beyond their customary models for fresh insight. This comes from the account of the outpouring of the Spirit on the day of Pentecost, and from what is known of the church of Corinth with its many gifts and ministries, all coming from the one and the same Spirit. Prophets, moreover, are seen to have had a role in shaping the canon of scriptures used in common worship through interpretation of the scriptures and through the proclamation of Jesus as Lord. Teachers also by their gifts helped to gather and pass on the memoirs of the apostles. While these gifts of the Spirit had a special place in the early shaping of the tradition, they may continue to have a role in some form in worship today.

There is also a growing awareness that some free oral and bodily expression, within a credal and anamnetic framework, was a part of early practices of eucharist and blessing. This occurred indeed within a framework of anamnesis, or remembrance of God's great deeds culminating in Jesus Christ, and with an ear for correct credal expression, such as is given in the Apostles' Creed. Nonetheless, the earliest texts for blessing prayers of which we know were offered as guides rather than as rigorously set forms. With a stronger faith in the operation of the Spirit, such prayer could be offered with confidence in this inspiration, making a ready conjunction between the faith handed on and the present need and reality of community.[2]

Though there are definite limits, some readiness to accommodate moments of freely expressed prayer is found in the current liturgical books of the Catholic Church. In the Roman Missal, for example, though formulas are offered, it is indicated that the prayer of penitence, the prayer of the faithful and the selection of antiphons and hymns are open to the choice and composition of ministers within the gathered local community.

How all of this is to be incorporated into liturgy is scarcely a matter that has attained an easy consensus. Catholics would generally prefer to relate the term baptism in the Spirit to the sacrament of baptism by which adults and children are initiated into the church and into Christ, and not look to a baptism in the Spirit that comes later.[3] They believe that the promise of the life and gifts of the Spirit goes with the sacrament, and this promise is realized under the inspiration of the Spirit throughout life, even but not necessarily in deeply-felt moments of conversion. It is easier to incorporate this perception into a living faith in adult catechumenate and baptism than into infant baptism. However, this too is seen as the beginning of life of growth in the ways of the Spirit, in the following of Jesus Christ.

Theologically and practically, better appreciation is needed of the prophetic that undercuts the rigidity of set forms. Many, however, prefer to understand this chiefly in terms of an interpretation that relates God's Word to the present, and give less emphasis to gifts, such as praying with tongues. The charismatic movement within Catholicism has raised more insistently the question of the expectation of the prophetic gifts that goes with baptism. Its members would see this as something to be experienced later in life, though still having its roots in the initial reception of the sacrament of baptism. In another area of prayer, cultures that have retained traditions of gifted healers and healing are asking how these may be recognized and incorporated into worship, as a sign of the activity of the Spirit and of the presence of God's kingdom. There is still much discussion among Catholics around these points and their pertinence to common worship. Greater dialogue and contact with Pentecostals will be of value in this regard.

II. Body and worship

Sacramentality is the core of Catholic worship, and something that was strongly defended at the time of the Reformation. Catholic liturgy embodies the belief that the gift of grace and the experience of divine presence is mediated through earthly elements and bodily mediation, employed in faith in keeping remembrance of the Word Incarnate. An Augustinian formula readily adopted is that the four basic sacramental signs of Christian worship are bread, wine, oil and water, together with the laying-on of hands. Being basic elements of human existence and of humanity's oneness with the earth, they are also basic elements in mediating the gift and community of the Spirit. In remembrance of Christ, in proclaiming him as Lord of all things, and in the power of the Spirit, the body is washed, anointed and nourished as it is caught up in the rhythm of ritual action. Blessing of those elements, and of those who use them, has its foundations in Judaism, with its blessings for fruits of the earth, and its petitions for the land, and for healing of body, mind and spirit. God is blessed for the gifts, and the gifts are so blessed by God that they become the mediating force of life and Spirit.

In the course of time, some Neoplatonic dualism and some mechanical instrumentalist thinking have clouded over the Spirit-filled nature of the use of bodily elements and actions. Nonetheless, there remains the persuasion that God comes to believers and sanctifies them through the body, and heals persons in 'body, mind and spirit'. In the eucharist, God is believed to offer the flesh of Christ and the gift of the Spirit to believers in sacramental form, 'for the forgiveness of sins and the gift of immortality', raising up believers now in body and spirit in the hope of the final resurrection. This indeed is the heart of Catholic liturgy. The belief in the communion of the living and the dead, in eschatological hope, or even trust in relics of saints, is part of this body-centred spirituality, engendered by sacrament and ritual. Catholics find a ready resonance with the words of Irenaeus when he says of belief in the goodness of creation and the resurrection of the body, 'our opinion agrees with the eucharist and the eucharist in turn confirms our opinion'.[4]

For all of this, it has to be granted that the bodily expression of Catholic liturgy tends to be that of formal ritualized movement, though in recent decrees on inculturation there is more attention to the bodily movement that pervades the entire action of worship, and this is seen and heard more readily in the accommodations of an African heritage. The reason for placing the accent on formal ritual action is the perceived coincidence between the person-body and the social body. Body experience in worship is that of the person within the corporate or communal tradition and movement, with which each and all are associated in a very personal way through liturgical action.

What prevails is the sense of the body as the bearer of tradition, of a passing on of traditions and of life-forces through learned bodily rituals, which make one with learned story, creed and prayer. This concerted action incorporates persons and communities into a living tradition that encompasses history and social belonging. Thus the bodily nature of baptism and the eucharist, and bodily effects experienced in anointing and healing, are seen as elements of incorporation into Christ's mystery, through the action of the Spirit, and as elements forming the church into the sign of the kingdom of God.

III. Worship and kingdom

In line with this, there is a need for Catholics to come to a better appreciation of the fact that all worship is witness to the kingdom inaugurated in Jesus Christ. For this to be more vividly felt, communities have to incorporate living witness into their liturgies in a more generous fashion. The foundation of Catholic veneration of the saints is belief in their witness to Jesus Christ, and the continuation of this witness and of a living communion with them in their remembrance. The risk of this is that witness may be placed too much in the past, especially since the canonization process takes a long time. Popular devotion, however, counters this by its own attention to the present time. Catholic peoples recognize today's martyrs in persons such as Oscar Romero, and venerate them without need of formal official recognition. In so doing, they associate their memory with living movements and actions that continue as witness to Jesus Christ and his Spirit, even in the face of the evils of the time in which we live.

It is true, however, that Catholics put less crisis-development dialectic into their view of salvation history than Pentecostals. This is because of a focus on tradition, institution and doctrine that is believed to be passed on in the name of Christ. It also goes with the point mentioned above, namely with the accent on the community of charity in the Spirit of Christ as itself the sign of the kingdom and the guarantor of its presence. Here also, however, there is a growing readiness to give a prophetic reading to remembrance of Jesus Christ and in this way to be more open to the dramatic elements in his passion and in the life of Christians generally. This goes with a reading of the signs of the times, finding in them the evil to be resisted and the work of the Spirit in various, often newly emerging, life-forces.

Conclusion

Perhaps these reflections on Catholic forms of worship, both as they have been passed on and as they are taking shape, may serve to show the comparisons and the contrasts between the Pentecostal prayer explained by Steven Land and the Catholic tradition. May they help towards greater mutual understanding and towards greater exchange and dialogue.

Notes

1. See the 1976 Report on Pentecostal-Roman Catholic Conversation, in *Growth in Agreement. Reports and Agreed Statements of Ecumenical Conversations on a World Level*, edited by Harding Meyer and Lukas Vischer, Geneva and New York 1984, 422–31.

2. On this the above-mentioned report has this to say: 'Public worship should safeguard a whole composite of elements: spontaneity, freedom, discipline, objectivity. On the Roman Catholic side, it was noted that the new revised liturgy allows for more opportunities for spontaneous prayer and singing at the Eucharist and in the rite of penance. The Pentecostal tradition has come to accept a measure of structure in worship and recognizes the development in its own history toward some liturgy', *Growth in Agreement* (n. 1), 427.

3. For areas of agreement and divergence, see the section on baptism in the above-mentioned report, ibid., 424–7.

4. *Adversus Haereses*, IV, 18, 4.

Born Again: Baptism and the Spirit

A Pentecostal Perspective

Juan Sepúlveda

I. Baptism in the Spirit as 'second blessing'

It is at present clearly established in academic literature that what distinguishes Pentecostalism, not only from the traditional Christian confessions, but also from *evangelicals* and *charismatics*, is the view of Baptism in the Holy Spirit as an additional experience, coming after conversion or initiation into Christian life, that is, as a 'second blessing'.

The theological course of this assumption, starting from John Wesley's doctrine of Christian perfection, moving through the linking of Christian perfection to the work of the Holy Spirit, as insinuated by John Fletcher and developed by the Holiness Movement in the United States, to the 'classic' formulation of Pentecostalism at the end of the last century, has been carefully studied by Donald Dayton.[1] The question of the New Testament basis for the doctrine of 'second blessing' has also been the subject of extensive investigation and discussion, especially since James Dunn subjected it to a rigorous exegetical examination in his famous work *Baptism in the Holy Spirit*.[2]

For Pentecostalists formed in a version of Pentecostalism whose tradition is basically oral, and also geographically and culturally isolated from what one might call the original context of the 'doctrinal evolution' of Pentecostalism, the huge amount of devotional and academic literature produced by the various protagonists of the historical course charted by

Dayton is surprising. Much the same could be said of the many pages written on whether or not the New Testament understood Baptism in the Holy Spirit as a second blessing or not. This abundant literature sheds a lot of light by which Pentecostalists of an oral tradition can situate themselves within the history and geneaological tree of Christian families, and at the same time suggests that Pentecostalism is not 'pure subjectivity', as many would say that it is.

This surprise, though, brings its own problems. The impression one is left with by the history related by Donald Dayton is – at the risk of caricaturing it – this: that groups of educated Christians from the United States and Great Britain, doubting whether their understanding of the plan of salvation was sufficiently orthodox, spent much of their time in prayer and systematic study in order to establish the correct interpretation, making use of numerous academic centres and publications to do so. Once they were convinced they had discovered a neglected dimension of the saving plan, a revival movement was set in motion to warn the ordinary members of the churches of this neglect, and to reach this neglected dimension through extraordinary efforts of prayer and devotion. If such a picture is accurate, then the experience seems to have been always secondary and subordinate to 'orthodoxy', and revival to have been the (technical?) mediator between orthodoxy and experience. The interminable debates on whether there were two blessings or three, or whether the Holy Spirit acted only in the final one or also in the first one (or two), seem to prove that 'right knowledge' had to come first, so as then to be applied to 'right experience'.

II. The view from Pentecostalism of the oral tradition

This impression probably derives partially from the lack of references in the literature to the specific human subjects of the process that led to the Pentecostal formulation: what were the biographical or existential circumstances, both personal and collective, that awakened doubts about understanding of the plan of salvation and, as a result, motivated revivals and their theological expressions? In any case, the point I want to stress here is that I find it quite difficult to relate the Pentecostal experience, as I have heard it told in many testimonies by Chilean Pentecostalists, to the doctrinal complications mentioned above. Put in another way, from a strictly formal perspective, the Pentecostalism in which I was brought up does not fit into the generally accepted pattern of Pentecostalism.

It is true that the 'original revival' of Chilean Pentecostalism (1902–10) follows a similar model: spiritual doubt or dissatisfaction; study and prayer in search of an answer, ending with the discovery of 'clear and definitive Baptism in the Holy Spirit . . . as something additional to justification and sanctification';[3] revival. It is also true that doctrinal articles translated from English and published in local Pentecostal journals repeat the classical formula, as do some pastors formed under the influence of foreign Pentecostal missions. However, for by far the greater part of Chilean Pentecostalism, the Pentecostal experience is summed up in one simple affirmation repeated time and again in 'testimonies': 'I met the Lord and he made me a *new being*'.[4]

This basic affirmation, with its many variants ('God changed my life', 'made me a new person', etc.), refers in narrative form to a founding experience that seems to unite the various dimensions that attempting to understand separates: the same experience is seen simultaneously as unconditional acceptance on the part of God (justification), as the beginning of a new life (sanctification), as reception of a new power to sustain new life in a hostile social and cultural environment, and as sharing and communicating this power to others (Baptism in the Holy Spirit?). This description would certainly be sufficient for an academic concerned with strict maintenance of accepted categories to catalogue it as *evangelical* rather than *Pentecostal*. Nevertheless, Acts 2 and John 3.1–15 (new birth = birth in the Spirit) are still the favourite biblical paradigms to which Chilean Pentecostalists resort to 'give a name' to their experience, and this is frequently, though not necessarily, accompanied by extraordinary (in the sense of not everyday) manifestations, such as speaking in tongues, dancing, visions, weeping, laughter, whose biblical paradigm is to be found in the 'gifts of the Spirit' (I Cor. 12.4–11, 28–30; Eph. 4.7–12). Certainly, in the self-understanding Chilean Pentecostalists have of their experience, God has come to meet them not only through proclamation of the Word: God the Father and his Son Jesus Christ have become present in real and active form through the Holy Spirit. There is, then, more than one reason to go on categorizing this experience as 'Pentecostal'.

III. Reinterpreting the metaphor of 'new birth'

As a contribution to the ecumenical debate which this issue seeks to promote, I should like to take this relatively 'heterodox' situation of Chilean Pentecostalism[5] as a 'vantage point' from which to recover two basic senses of the Pentecostal emphasis on *new birth = birth (Baptism) in the Spirit*. I do not mean to say that these senses are entirely absent from classical Pentecostal 'orthodoxy', but they have become too diluted in the midst of doctrinal distinctions.

The first sense has to do with the experience of *change*: being Christian produces a radical difference for the person concerned. 'Being Christian' cannot be put in the class of category, such as 'nationality' or 'culture', by which people identify with all those belonging to the society in which their biological birth takes place. Nor does it correspond to categories such as 'profession' or 'political affiliation', which, at least in modern society, also imply a certain personal change and decision, but rather to one that does not necessarily involve the whole person. Being Christian produces something completely new in a person, something that includes and reorders all other forms of identification, just as it also transforms relationships with oneself and with others.

This change certainly involves making a decision to change: that is, the decision to accept the call of the God who comes to meet us. But the change is not simply the result of our decision; it is made possible by the power of the Spirit working in us. Hence the importance of the theme of 'power': it is a matter of receiving the power, strength, energy, vitality, that we need to live in accordance with the will of God, which does not necessarily correspond to the values and life-styles we have received through our socialization process. For some, this change is perceived basically as a healing experience, that is, as an overcoming of personal situations that have blocked a life of fullness and love. For others, it is perceived as a liberating experience, as a force that allows them 'to stand up straight' and confront dependencies, structures and relationships that have oppressed their existence. For others yet, it is perceived as a powerful challenge summoning them to abandon a life of routine and egoism in favour of a life with purpose and open to God and neighbour.

This view evidently presupposes that 'being Christian' resolves a previous situation of lack or incompleteness that demands a change: the situation we call *sin* in theological terms. But to go talking in 'experiential' terms, I should say that for the majority of those who, in Chile, Latin America, and the rest of the world, have experienced their meeting with God through Pentecostalism, this situation demanding change could be described simply as one of *deep need*. This means that for most people, their personal history and the conditions of life in which they live are very far from representing the best of all possible worlds. For them, life is not something taken for granted, but rather something hard-won every day. And it is precisely the 'needy' to whom 'good news' makes sense: 'Those who are well have no need of the physician, but those who are sick', said Jesus (Mark 2.17 par.). And what of those who are satisfied, those who feel no need? According to the Gospels, for them the meeting with Jesus generally meant a huge challenge, which called into question the whole basis of their false security.

The second sense is an ecclesiological consequence of the first: being church also makes a radical difference. A system of Christendom or 'state church', handed down from the Constantinian era, does not correspond to the understanding of 'being Christian' presented above. Church is the open community of all those who have experienced renewal of their lives through the power of the Spirit. For Pentecostals, the church is the community that in the name of its Lord *invites, welcomes and sends out*. Through its invitation and sending out, the church as community of the Spirit shows its missionary dimension, which is inseparable from its identity. Through its welcome, the church makes manifest the restoring, healing and liberating power of the Spirit, giving each person and the community as a whole the strength to affirm new life and to take part in the mission of its Lord.

It is very likely that these two dimensions would also have operated as a basic underpinning of the revivals of the eighteenth and nineteenth centuries. Nevertheless, their theological formulation remained trapped within an excessively conceptual tradition. Logical imperatives ended by transforming what might be called different dimensions of the Christian experience into separate 'experiences'. The whole debate on the question of whether Luke-Acts recognizes a single conversion-initiation event or separate 'blessings' is complicated (or resolved?) by the certainty that Luke can never have asked such a question. As all experience is unrepeatable, it cannot be reduced to concepts. Metaphorical language – as when we speak of 'new birth' – is more adequate as an instrument for communicating the *newness* of the Christian experience and that of the faith community.

A final reflection

In the 'state church' model, or when 'free' churches adopt the style of that model, the rhythm of church life tends to be set by the 'satisfied', with the 'needy' being left on the margins. The 'needy' can be seen as objects of charity, but rarely as privileged subjects of church life. In this context, the upsurge of new forms of Christianity that emphasize 'new birth', whether they are strictly Pentecostal or not, can be interpreted not only as a movement of restoration of a more primitive model (New Testament and pre-Constantinian) of Christian experience, but also as a form of protest against a Christianity in which the 'needy' have been pushed to the margins.

Limitations of space have prevented me from tackling the subject of baptism with water in Christian and church experience. It needs to be said, though, that the complex of problems on the ecumenical level surrounding baptismal practices and the recourse to 're-baptism' is more a historical derivation from the system of Christendom in itself than a problem created by intents to 'reform' it. As Jürgen Moltmann has shown,[6] the baptismal practices of traditional Christianity are an inheritance from the Constantinian era.

Translated by Paul Burns

Notes

1. D. Dayton, *Theological Roots of Pentecostalism*, Grand Rapids 1987.
2. J. D. G. Dunn, *Baptism in the Holy Spirit*, London 1971. A continuation of the dialogue between Dunn and Pentecostal academics can be found in *Journal of Pentecostal Theology* 3 (1993), 4 (1994) and 6 (1995).
3. W. Hoover, *Historia del avivamiento pentecostal en Chile*, Valparaiso 1948, 14.
4. Cf Canales, Palma and Villela, *En tierra extraña II*, Santiago 1991, 59–74; J. Sepúlveda, 'Pentecostalism as Popular Religiosity', *International Review of Mission* 309, 1989, 80–8.
5. Although I cannot prove it in detail, I have the impression that this position of 'heterodoxy' is shared by many of the Pentecostal groups of the (till recently) so-called Third World.
6. J. Moltmann, *The Church in the Power of the Spirit*, London 1977, 226–42.

A Protestant Response

James D. G. Dunn

It is important to recognize how much the debate about baptism and the Spirit has developed. At the beginning of the present century, classic Pentecostalism posed two particular issues to traditional theology and church by its two most distinctive teachings: 1. baptism in the Spirit as a second experience of empowering subsequent to conversion (and baptism), a second experience which all Christians should seek for themselves; 2. baptism in the Spirit as attested by the sign of speaking in tongues. Now, following a cycle which has run through several phases, particularly in the English-speaking world (Neo-Pentecostalism, charismatic renewal, house church movement, Vineyard churches and Toronto blessing), the issues have become significantly different. Issues of 'second blessing' and speaking in tongues have been largely side-lined, to be replaced by questions about signs and wonders, and about the character of (and checks on) charismatic leadership and authority.

Nevertheless, the earlier issues still remain important, not least because the influence of Pentecostal-type experience(s) and teaching has spread far more widely than the English-speaking world. Consequently, the earlier issues are still live issues in many parts of the world. Moreover, the experience of spiritual renewal is bound to raise questions regarding ecclesiastical, liturgical and theological traditions which have failed to deliver that experience for so many seekers after God. What, then, is to be learned from this spread of 'Pentecostal experience' and the ecclesiastical tensions and theological debates it has provoked? Let me suggest a few from a New Testament and (primarily) Protestant perspective.

I. The importance of experience

No one need or should doubt that theological reflection, ecclesiastical practice and personal experience have to go hand in hand in a rounded Christian confession. Here it is the lively experience of grace as the wellspring of faith and common life which calls for particular attention. The history of Christianity's beginnings, not least in Acts and the New Testament letters, bears abundant testimony to this: 'the fellowship of the Spirit' is first and foremost 'the shared experience of the Spirit' (this is primarily a matter of correct translation of the Greek). But Christian history reminds us, if we needed reminding, both how dangerous an emphasis on experience can be, and how easy it is for a vital personal experience of God to be subordinated to and lost sight of behind concern for ecclesiastical authority and theological propriety.

Here the whole Pentecostal phenomenon has to be credited for reminding the traditional churches of the importance of this dimension in Christian faith and life. This is the undeniable force of the multitudinous personal testimonies on the subject – of the first Pentecostals, of Chilean Pentecostals today, of individuals who have become alive in the Spirit/spirit through the charismatic renewal while remaining within older ecclesiastical traditions, and so on. The dimension of personal experience within the totality of Christian discipleship is ignored to our common peril and impoverishment.

More fundamental still, Juan Sepúlveda's critique of Dayton and his account of the beginnings of Chilean Pentecostalism reflect the importance of the 'founding experience' in earliest Christianity also. In the beginning was experience; the living root of Christianity (as of religion generally) is the experience of God's Spirit. In an important sense doctrine is the rationalization of the founding experience and church is the corporate expression and ordering of such experience; a Christianity which forgets this needs to read again Ezek. 37 and the account of Pentecost (Acts 2). Perhaps we should also add: unity grows out of the shared experience of the Spirit; an ecumenism which forgets or disregards this is doomed to failure.

II. 'A rose by any other name . . . '

The value of 'the Pentecostal experience' to the universal church has been diminished by the disputes it occasioned regarding both its form and its theological significance.

In the first case, classic Pentecostalism made the mistake of deducing from many specific experiences a general rule: that speaking in tongues is the sign of the Pentecostal experience. This deduction was made despite the fact that the full range of individual experiences attested were by no means so uniform, and despite the limited nature of the support given to the deduction from the New Testament (three episodes in Acts, without any obvious confirmation from the rest of the New Testament). The weakness of the biblical support and the continuing diversity of actual experiences of renewal have been major factors in the steady diminution in the importance of this issue, despite the continuing attraction of the teaching on tongues as the 'initial sign' in the neo-Pentecostal phase of the twentieth-century Pentecostalist phenomenon and in those movements elsewhere in the world more directly influenced by classic Pentecostal teaching as such.

More important has been the identification of the Pentecostal experience as 'baptism in the Spirit'. For this seemed to call in question (and in many formulations of the claim did in fact call in question) both the significance of conversion and baptism as the beginning of the Christian life and the presence of the Spirit in the life of the Christian who lacked the Pentecostal experience. The implicit élitism and consequent divisiveness of such claims have been prominent among the less welcome features of the whole affair. However, here too the course of the century has seen a steady weakening of the original Pentecostal theological assertion on this point.

On the one hand, at the level of theological debate as evidenced, for example, by the recently founded *Journal of Pentecostal Theology*, the weakness of the biblical support for a full-blown theology of subsequence has been acknowledged from within the Pentecostal tradition. First, by recognition that Paul's theology of Christian initiation is quite opposed to such a theology, as evidenced above all by the classic text, I Cor. 12.13 – 'baptized in one Spirit into one body'. The very imagery of baptism, as practised from the first, and as used by Paul to speak of integration into Christ and his death, can hardly be other than initiatory.

Secondly, by recognition that even in Acts the emphasis in the key passages (Acts 1; 2; 8; 10–11; 19) is on empowering and prophesying, but not on these as distinct from and subsequent to conversion-initiation. Even within more traditional Pentecostalism, therefore, the issue of subsequence has been recognized to be something of a red herring. And with that recognition, much of the heat has gone out of the debate on whether 'baptism in the Spirit' is a distinct act of the Spirit subsequent to conversion and initiation.

As the whole movement, or sequence of movements, has broadened out from the classic Pentecostalist base, the problems posed by a theology of Spirit baptism have also diminished. The term itself has become less prominent, as issues of charismatic gifts and ordering of worship and authority have assumed greater importance. Perhaps one could say, by way of generalization, that it is the vitality of experience of the Spirit which has been seen to be more important than the name given to it or the theology related to it. Here again the witness of the New Testament writers can be appealed to with good effect. For while they bear clear witness to the importance of experiencing the Spirit (including the experience of Christ as Lord and God as Father), they give no support whatsoever to the view that there is a specifically second experience of a particular character which all believers should expect and seek for as of right.

The clearing away of such distracting issues has the bonus of allowing the dynamic character of the initiating experience of the Spirit to come to the fore. This is clear, for example, from the context in which Paul places his talk of Spirit baptism (I Cor. 12.13), namely Spirit baptism as the equipping of the members of the body for charismatic service within the body. And Juan Sepúlveda's emphasis on the experience of 'new birth' as an experience of *change* and commission, and as giving the needy a voice and the marginalized a proper role, appropriately underlines the same point. Here, too, it has to be said, therefore, that Pentecostalism is the part of the world church which is giving most serious attention and effect to the ideal of 'the ministry of the whole people of God' affirmed so widely and enacted so feebly elsewhere.

III. Matching experience to doctrine and ritual

All that having been said, however, the whole phenomenon of the Pentecostal experience continues to pose at least two important theological and ecclesiastical issues which need repeatedly to be addressed.

One is the issue put so effectively by Juan Sepúlveda – 'giving a name' to the experience. It is easy to forget how many of our technical theological terms began as metaphors (salvation, justification, new birth, and so on), metaphors attempting to give expression to the reality of a widespread experience of grace which called in question established tenets and practices of mother Judaism. The first Christians seem to have ransacked their vocabulary in the attempt to express the richness and diversity of their experience of grace. But traditional theology has tended to transform these metaphors into technical terms, where the metaphor has died. Instead of providing a partial window into the experience of grace, and a means of expressing the vitality of that experience, the metaphors have lost their window-likeness and become more like window-less rooms within which experience is more likely to sicken and die than to thrive and flourish; or, to recall a dominical metaphor, like old, dried up wine-skins unable to contain the vitality of renewed experiences of grace.

The challenge, then, is whether the vitality of contemporary experience of the Spirit should be expected still to find appropriate expression in the metaphors of another age. Still more, whether the vitality of contemporary experience, Pentecostal or otherwise, should be expected to conform to the traditional (and dessicated) metaphors which have now become the technical terms of sound doctrine. As Pentecostal (and other) testimonies show, and as the previous article reminds us, the experience of renewal in the Spirit/spirit is often an experience just like those of the first Christians – that is, an experience searching for fresh and appropriate language to express its existential power. In such cases, to rule out certain metaphors in description of the experience or to require certain other metaphors in describing the experience can be among the most unsympathetic and suffocating responses which anyone rejoicing in the Spirit can receive. In such cases, both pastorally and theologically, the reminting of old metaphors (even baptism in the Spirit!) should not be dismissed out of hand, and the minting of fresh metaphors (still able to function as windows for today) should be encouraged. Here too Juan

Sepúlveda's reminder that 'the righteous' (sure of their doctrine, and content with their experience) need to remember that the word of grace is for 'sinners'.

The other issue is the question of the correlation of experience and sacrament. Anyone who has had dealings with those rejoicing in one or other of the manifestations of the Pentecostal experience will be aware of how powerful and poignant this issue is. Young people in particular, in their teens and twenties, who have experienced a quickening of the Spirit/spirit, have often longed for an appropriate sacramental expression of their experience. For those who had not previously been baptized, there is no problem. The rich symbolism of baptism, particularly as expounded by Paul, satisfies the deep need for a rite of passage from old life to new. But for those already baptized as children the situation can be totally frustrating. They do not recognize their previous baptism as existentially theirs; the theological rationalization which elides the difference of decades and generations does not satisfy the deep spiritual need for a ritual acknowledgement of the significance of the recent experience as *theirs*. The alternatives of confirmation or first communion or other contrived options have too little of the rich symbolism and emotional satisfaction provided by total immersion.

One cannot but warm to such desire for a sacramental expression of the experience of grace, a wholly welcome and proper recognition of the power of the symbol. Such a desire is itself the root of sacramental theology and practice; we cannot ignore it without ultimately calling in question the reality of sacramental grace itself (is the reception of grace always unconscious, to be deduced from proper administration of the sacrament, and never consciously experienced?). But those charged with safeguarding the church's traditions have naturally shied away from acceding to the request for a second baptism. The New Testament nowhere gives precedent for a repeated baptism in the name of Christ (contrast Acts 8.1–17 with 19.1–7). And the once-for-allness symbolized by baptism is too important an expression of the gospel to be lightly discarded. It is true that some denominations have toyed with the idea of a baptism-like ritual (baptism in all but name) to mark such powerful (once-for-all?) experiences of renewal. Most, however, have shied away from such a solution – but without solving the problem. It may yet come to a choice between preserving a sound doctrine and practice of baptism or losing the young people whose experience of grace does not fit with sacramental tradition – a choice already made by many individuals to the older traditions' loss.

If the New Testament is of any help here it is to provide a warning on both sides: do not give too much importance to the ritual moment and act. The teaching on this subject underwritten by all the principal New

Testament writers (John, Acts and Paul) boils down to this: the gift of the Spirit is tied no more tightly to baptism than it was to circumcision. This is certainly a warning to contemporary guardians of tradition: do not make the mistake over baptism which the early Jewish Christians made over circumcision; recognize and acknowledge the experience of grace wherever it occurs and work out from that (cf. Acts 15.6–29; Gal. 2.6–10). But it is equally a warning to those rejoicing in a new or renewed life in the Spirit: Is the church there solely to service your experience? Do not make the mistake of overvaluing God's gift to you (cf. I Cor. 4.6–8; II Cor. 12.1–10).

Only the most churlish or pedantic traditionalist could fail to rejoice in the reinvigoration of spiritual experience claimed and attested within the third stream of Christianity, at present most fully represented by Pentecostalism in its various phases. Of course the affirmation and welcome are bound to include some questionings and qualifications; no one who is aware of the history of the third stream of Christianity could doubt that. But that affirmation and welcome can be whole-hearted only if the issues which the third stream poses to the older church are given proper recognition and respect, analogous to the recognition and respect which each denomination now expects for its own traditions within ecumenical discussion. And high among these issues is the unresolved question: does our present theology and liturgy give appropriate expression to the experience of the Spirit to which twentieth-century Pentecostalism bears such powerful witness?

Discerning Who Builds the Church: A Catholic Response

Michel Quesnel

The presentation of baptism in the Spirit as a second blessing or, to put things a different way, as a rite sanctioning the second conversion, is certainly an approach which can prompt the Catholic Church to engage in some useful reflection. The description which has just been given of

Chilean Pentecostalism shows that such a baptism corresponds to a real need in popular circles, and that it is sometimes the only way by which these circles are linked with the church today. However, if we are to evaluate how well founded it is, we need to ask two types of question. First, doesn't such a rite duplicate sacraments or sacramentals which already exist? And secondly, as it is practised in Pentecostal tendencies today, does it correspond to the usually accepted criteria for a rite which is accepted as Catholic? If the answer to these two questions leads to a favourable verdict on baptism in the Spirit, we shall, finally, be able to examine what it could bring to the Catholic Church and the other churches, and to the advancement of ecumenism.

I. Other rites of second blessing

With its seven sacraments and the profusion of its rites, at first sight the Catholic Church might seem to need a rite like that of baptism in the spirit less than any other church. There is a specific sacrament for every step, or almost every step, of the Christian life, and neither those who receive a sacrament nor the theologians themselves have completely exhausted its riches. Two of these sacraments in a way play the role of a second baptism: confirmation, and the sacrament of penitence or reconciliation.

Christian initiation is celebrated in three stages: baptism, confirmation and the eucharist – traditionally in that order. In fact the age of reception of confirmation has varied over the centuries. In numerous countries today, particularly in Western Europe, confirmation has become the sacrament of adolescence or post-adolescence, and the traditional order has given place to a new one: baptism, eucharist, confirmation.

The person who receives confirmation ten or fifteen years after baptism sometimes feels it as an acceptance of the baptism received at a tender age which is both more aware and more rooted in the ecclesial community. In the *Catechism of the Catholic Church* promulgated in 1992, which here takes up Vatican II, we read: 'By the sacrament of Confirmation, the baptized are more perfectly bound to the Church and are enriched with a special strength of the Holy Spirit. Hence they are, as true witnesses of Christ, more strictly obliged to spread and defend the faith by word and deed.'' In this sense, confirmation can seem well placed to play the role of 'second blessing' or be a rite of second conversion, which is how the Pentecostalists see baptism in the Spirit.

However, on examination we have to recognize that such a presentation is partly theoretical. Certainly a young person of between fifteen and eighteen can see the confirmation that he or she has received as consecrating a personal commitment to the faith, almost as a second baptism at the beginning of adulthood; in that case confirmation plays a role close to that of baptism in the Spirit. But it has to be recognized that often, when confirmation is presented as an indispensable stage in the completion of Catholic initiation, it does not play this role. The very fact that it is part of a programme robs it of the dimension of personal freedom which is emphasized by the Pentecostal rite. One is converted because one is grasped by God in an unforeseeable way, not to order; conversion cannot be programmed.

However, there is another sacrament in the Catholic Church which is much better than confirmation in taking account of the disposition of the subject, and which honours his or her readiness to be converted: the sacrament of penitence and reconciliation. In the time of Constantine, moreover, it was considered as a kind of second baptism which could not be repeated. For fear of then lapsing into sin with no possibility of forgiveness, people ended up by delaying its reception as late as possible before death, and in a way it became a passport to eternity.[2]

This practice in fact indicates how much the desire for a second baptism or a second blessing cannot be satisfied by the Catholic sacrament of reconciliation. While one of its effects is common with that of baptism, namely the forgiveness of sins, the reflection of the church and of theologians has always presented it primarily as a rite aimed at removing faults rather than renewing the positive side of the baptismal condition: justification, sanctification, the active power of the Spirit.

At the end of a convoluted history, the positive force of the sacrament is being emphasized more during the twentieth century; the very fact that the aim of reconciliation is tending to replace that of penitence is an illustration of this. However, we must recognize that individual wishes and individual absolution limit the ecclesial scope of the sacrament, and that it has not completely lost its dimension of being a 'spiritual detergent', lacking many of the features common to the joyful festivals which accompany the celebrations of baptism in the Spirit.

After this brief examination of the two sacraments which could be cited by way of comparison, we have to admit that in the classical theology of the Catholic Church there is no rite which has effects comparable to those of baptism in the Spirit. There is room for a 'second benediction' which consecrates an effective conversion of the subject.

II. The baptism of the Spirit and discerning the spirits

Once it has been recognized that there is a ritual void in the Catholic Church which needs to be filled if the second conversion is to be honoured, we need to check to see whether the baptism in the Spirit as practised by Pentecostals can fill this place. So there is a need to use discernment, which is traditionally called 'discernment of the spirit'. Seven or eight criteria are usually employed to check whether movements or inspirations are in conformity with the divine will. Here is the list as it appears in a spiritual encyclopaedia which is currently being published: truth, seriousness or usefulness, intellectual light, discretion and moderation, humility accompanied by docility and trust, peace, purity of intention, abandonment to Our Lord.[3] Without taking these criteria up one by one, we can at least see whether or not baptism in the Spirit corresponds generally to them.

The first check to make is that of truth. Is there justification for, if not direct attestation of, such a rite in the Bible, and more specifically in the New Testament? It is not easy to answer this question. J. D. G. Dunn, whose book, which is already quite an old one, was warmly welcomed by the Pentecostalists, answers it in the affirmative.[4] The first general Catholic study, by two North Americans, Frs McDonnell and Montague, who themselves belong to the Renewal, equally gives a positive response.[5] The opinion of non-Pentecostalist exegetes is more differentiated.[6] The practice by the disciples of a rite of the imposition of hands aimed at the outpouring of the Spirit and at a long distance from baptism with water is possible according to the New Testament, but not cleaarly attested; the most open text in this connection is the mission command to the apostles in the Gospel of Mark: ' . . . he began to send them out two by two, giving them authority over unclean spirits' (Mark 6.7); however, there is no indication of any action to perform. That having been said, all the sacraments of the church are far from being materially prescribed by Jesus in the scriptures; there is nothing there about baptism in the Spirit, and there is nothing in the texts which tells against it either.

As a correlative to this criterion of truth, there is that of seriousness and usefulness for the church. In other words, is the baptism in the Spirit given 'for edification', to take up St Paul's expression (I Cor. 14.26), or not? Furthermore, the apostle puts forward this demand for the building up of the body of the church in connection with the discernment to be used among the different charisms. Here we have to recognize that the response is clearly positive. There was a time when the Catholic Church regarded the charismatic communities with real mistrust, and the Catholic Pentecostals felt almost compelled to leave the church. However, this time is past. Certainly there must be continued vigilance towards possible excesses: the renewal must not encourage among its members a mistrust of pastors who are ill at ease in this sensibility, or create parallel hierarchies. But in the majority of places a legitimate circumspection has replaced reciprocal mistrust, and we can only rejoice at this, in the name of the pluralism which must have a place within the church.

One might have more reservations over the functioning of the criterion of discretion and moderation. What disturbs a large number of classical Christians in charismatic gatherings is the place occupied in them by emotions and the often excessive character of the celebrations. This was already denounced by St Paul in the assemblies in Corinth (I Cor. 12–14). Here it is particularly important to show sensitivity, which differs from one latitude to another. On the other hand, we might ask ourselves whether the freedom of behaviour to the rhythm of the Spirit as practised in Renewal groups does not pose useful questions to Christians accustomed to well-behaved, perhaps too well-behaved, celebrations. Are these interesting the faithful less and less? Here, too, a frank dialogue can avoid blocks.

Furthermore, it cannot be said that Christians who practise baptism in the Spirit lack either purity of intention or abandonment to our Lord. In numerous countries, it is above all among the marginalized that this practice has emerged, whereas the officials of the church usually belong to the governing class; the life of Pentecostal groups often has an air of authentic popular religion. It is true that particularly in Western Europe the Renewal is now affecting many quite middle-class areas, and that the temptation for certain favoured groups to send their legions to restore a church which is to their taste is not illusory. But we should not generalize about these manipulative intentions, which can be a characteristic of any pressure group.

III. Conclusion

At the end of this survey, Catholic theologians are led to recognize that baptism in the Spirit is a practice which puts questions to their church. The rite is related on the one hand to confirmation in its dimension of second blessing, and secondly to the sacrament of reconciliation in its dimension of second conversion. What is original about it as compared with the classical sacraments of initiation is that its moment is freely chosen by the subject in terms of her or his personal journey. Catholic theology, putting emphasis on the permanent gift of God which is bestowed on us through the sacraments and is mistrustful of excessive subjectivity, has sometimes given the sacraments an almost timeless or impersonal character with a universal force. Certainly the restoration of an approach in terms of the subject is one of its tasks.

Baptism in the Spirit has not appeared in the churches through the voice of its authorities – the rite comes 'from the base' and a pyramidal

Catholicism is not spontaneously open to this type of emergence. But when one looks at some of the seven sacraments and a large number of other Catholic rites of yesterday and today, doesn't history show us that things have often come about in this way? A need of the faithful is identified, a practice exists, sometimes even of pagan origin. The church allows itself to be asked questions, the theologians reflect, the magisterium discerns, abolishes, encourages or reorientates. The hierarchy has been charged to teach, sanctify and govern in the name of Christ.[7] Its function is not to invent everything.

Today, the question of baptism in the Spirit is being raised simultaneously in several Christian confessions. Hasn't an opportunity been given to the churches to study it together and see if there isn't a way of unity here?

Translated by John Bowden

Notes

1. *Catechism of the Catholic Church*, 1285; *Lumen Gentium*, 11.
2. C. Vogel, *Le pécheur et la pénitence dans l'Église ancienne*, Paris 1966.
3. 'Discernement des esprits', *Catholicisme* III, 1951, 874–7.
4. J. D. G. Dunn, *Baptism in the Holy Spirit*, London 1970.
5. K. McDonnell and G. T. Montague, *Christian Initiation and Baptism in the Holy Spirit*, Collegeville 1991. The work analyses the patristic writings as well as the New Testament.
6. Cf. my contribution to a colloquium organized at the Institut catholique de Paris by the Communauté du Chemin neuf, published in *Tychique* 114, March 1995, 3–23, and in the *Revue de l'Institut catholique de Paris* 54 (April-June 1995), 47–63.
7. *Catechism of the Catholic Church*, 888–896.

III · Synthesis

Pentecost and the Theology of Life

Jürgen Moltmann

The dialogues in this issue show that there are only a few fundamental differences between the traditional churches and the new Pentecostal churches, while they have much in common. There are very different perspectives, but these are perspectives on a shared concern. So in this synthesis article I do not want to recapitulate the small syntheses but to look at that great synthesis which is coming into being today both ecumenically and all over the world under the phrase 'theology of life'.

Life today is in deadly danger as never before. Since Hiroshima in 1945 the human race has become mortal. In a secular sense we exist in the end-time, i.e. in a time in which the end of life is possible at any moment as a result of modern mass means of destruction (nuclear, biological and chemical weapons).[1] We cannot imagine a time when this threat which humankind poses to itself will no longer exist, since the formulae for the powers of destruction cannot be forgotten again. Since Chernobyl in 1986 we have been aware that the earth can be made uninhabitable by contamination, as that region in White Russia and the Ukraine has been made uninhabitable for decades. The man-made ecological devastations of the earth, the water and the air are spreading as humankind, its industrialization and urbanization increase, and do not just destroy human life. The modern world produces surplus people who are exposed to an early death: through the abortion of unborn life, through neglect of the 'street children', through adult women and men who are unemployed, and through disease as a result of the return of epidemics to those lands suffering starvation. The globalization of capital and the markets is making more and more people superfluous. At present Africa is the forgotten continent.[2]

The 'theology of life' is coming into being ecumenically and world-wide. To mention just a few examples: as the composite volume *Mysterium Liberationis* (1990) shows, the Latin American theology of liberation is developing further into a 'theology of life' and of the kingdom of God.[3] In 1993 the Commission on Unity III of the World Council of Churches in Geneva resolved on a study programme on 'the theology of life' after the Korean theologian Chung Hyun Hyung had called for a new 'culture of life' in her striking lecture at the WCC conference in Canberra in 1991.[4] In Germany there are new discoveries around the 'theology of hope' on the way to a new theology of the Holy Spirit.[5] The ecological theologies of e.g. Rosemary Ruether and Leonardo Boff are increasingly strongly perceiving human life in the web of all living creatures and are encouraging a new bioethics.[6] Not least, reference should be made to John Paul II's encyclical of 30 March 1995, *Evangelium Vitae*. The theological commitment to the Christian experience of Pentecost should make an integral theology of life possible, in which the different confessions and denominations come together to follow the divine mission of life.

I. The expectation and coming of the Holy Spirit

Prayers to the Holy Spirit are all grounded in the prayer for the coming of the Spirit. The coming of the Spirit is something special, and in the Christian tradition it is called the *epiclesis* of the Spirit. Most hymns for Pentecost only exclaim 'Come, Holy Spirit' (*Veni, Creator Spiritus*, Hrabanus Maurus). The prayer for the Holy Spirit is directed toward its comprehensive presence. The Spirit is more than just one gift among others; the Holy Spirit is the unlimited presence of God in which our lives are quickened and awakened to new life and given the powers of the Spirit. The prayers for the coming of the Holy Spirit are Maranatha prayers. As is well known, Maranatha prayers are directed to Christ and are eschatological in meaning: 'Amen. Come, Lord Jesus!' is the next to the last saying in the New Testament (Rev. 22.20). However, here, too, not only the person of Jesus is meant, but his coming in the glory of God to create the world anew. The parousia of the Holy Spirit is nothing other than the beginning of the parousia of Christ. Thus the Holy Spirit is called the 'pledge' of glory (Eph. 1.14; II Cor. 1.22). What is beginning in the Holy Spirit here will be consummated in the kingdom of glory there. The kingdom of glory does not come unexpected and unprepared; it proclaims its coming in the kingdom of the Spirit and takes control of the present in it.

In praying for the coming of the Spirit, those who pray open themselves to expectation and let the energies of the Spirit flow into their lives. Even when humans can still only groan for salvation and in their groaning fall silent, God's Spirit is already groaning in them and interceding for them

(Rom. 8.26). Praying and groaning for God's Spirit to come into this life of imprisonment and this devastated world are its first signs of life from the Holy Spirit as Frank Macchia has shown.

We experience the Holy Spirit again and again in two ways: as a divine Other to whom we call, and as divine Presence in which we call. This is not unusual. As children we experienced our mother in two ways: as presence that surrounds us, and as other that calls us.[7]

The response to the prayer for the Holy Spirit is the Spirit's coming and staying, being poured out and indwelling in us (*shekhingh*). Those who pray for the Holy Spirit to come to us, into our hearts, into our community and to our earth do not want to flee to heaven or be removed to the great beyond. They have hope for their hearts, their community and this earth. We do not pray, 'Let us come into your kingdom . . . ' We pray, 'Your kingdom come . . . on earth as it is in heaven.' Great, unbroken affirmation of life lies behind this prayer for the divine Spirit to come to us fragile and earthly human beings.

Another response to the prayer for the Holy Spirit is the 'outpouring of the Spirit on all flesh' (Joel 2.28; Acts 2.17ff.). What does this astounding metaphor say to us? 'All flesh' means human life first of all, but it also includes – as Gen. 9.10ff. says – all living things: plants, trees and animals. God himself is called 'the fountain of life' in Ps. 36.10. Jesus tells the Samaritan woman in John 4.14 that he will give her 'water' that flows from the spring of eternal life. The image of 'the fountain of life' and of water that gives life to everything that is withered and dried up is used to help us understand how the Holy Spirit works: as the 'water of life' the Spirit gives life and fruit to everything that dries up and dies.

The amazing thing about this is that the Holy Spirit is not regarded here as a divine person, but rather as the divine element. The Spirit is 'sent', and 'comes', but like a flood spreads out over all living things and penetrates everything. If the Holy Spirit is the special presence of God, then all flesh is deified in the 'outpouring of the Spirit of God'. All mortal flesh is filled with God's eternal life. For what comes from God is divine and eternal like God himself. In the 'outpouring of the Spirit of God' the deity reveals itself and becomes 'that divine power which pours and flows', as the mystic Mechthild of Magdeburg wrote. Whether at the source, in a river or in a sea, the water has the same quality, but different degrees of movement. The transition of the Spirit itself to the many assorted powers of the Spirit, from the *charis* to the *charismata*, is gradual. The divine becomes the inclusive presence in which humankind, indeed all living things, can develop fruitfully and live eternally (Ps. 139).

II. Origin and communication of the Holy Spirit

The question of the origin of the Holy Spirit is not a speculative question. It is a necessary one, because the end is implicit in the origin. The Holy Spirit brings and communicates that out of which it originates. So where does the Holy Spirit come from?

1. The shining countenance of God

The answer of the Old Testament is surprising. 'Do not drive me from your countenance or take your holy spirit from me', we pray with Ps. 51.11. And with Ps. 104.29ff. we recognize that in reference to all living things: 'Then you hide your face, and they are restless and troubled; when you take away your breath [spirit], they fail and they return to the dust from which they came; but when you breathe into them, they recover; you give new life to the earth.'

The 'countenance of God' is a symbol for God's turning to take care of us, God's attentive watch and God's special presence.[8] Everywhere we look, a person's face reveals what a person is really feeling inside: offence and joy, laughing and crying show themselves on our faces. We can transfer this observation in a similar manner to God's countenance. The 'hidden countenance' of God is regarded as a symbol of God's judgment in Jewish thought; when God averts his countenance that is regarded as a symbol for rejection by God and eternal death. The 'shining countenance' of God, however, is the source of the outpouring of the Spirit and the source of life itself, of love and divine blessing. 'The Lord make his countenance to shine upon you/us, and be gracious to you/us', we pray in the Aaronic blessing (Num. 4.24ff.). That is the prayer for the Holy Spirit, the extraordinary presence of God with us which quickens all living things.

When does a countenance 'shine'? When human faces look with love in their eyes, those faces begin to shine. When a mother takes her child in her arms and loves it, one sees her eyes shining. When one person wants to give another person a wonderful present, his or her eyes shine with excitement. Such 'radiant eyes' bring joy. We can imagine all this and more when we think of God's 'shining countenance' and look for the light of the Holy Spirit there. Confidence in our life and new vitality awaken in us when God looks at us with his joyous, shining eyes. The face of God that glows with joy is the light source of the Holy Spirit. His light floods us, and our faces become mirrors which reflect and spread this light.

According to Paul, the glory of God lights up the 'face of Christ' and has 'shone in our hearts' (II Cor. 4.6). Then we, too, shall reflect the glory of the Lord 'with unveiled face' (II Cor. 3.18). Our 'hidden face' is responsible for our not knowing ourselves; our true selves, how and what we really are, are hidden from us. Our desire for self-encounter and self-knowledge have their origin in this isolation, and will not be fulfilled until the arrival of the apocalypse which comes to be in 'seeing' God 'face to face' (I Cor. 13.12). Experience with the Spirit is that 'bright glow in our hearts' with which the apocalypse of our self begins.

2. The cross and resurrection of Christ

In the New Testament the Holy Spirit emerges out of the events in the story of Christ, the salvation history, that we celebrate in the liturgical year: Christmas – Good Friday – Easter – Ascension – Pentecost. Pentecost is the last feast in this series and thus the goal of the other feasts.

We see at first glance how the story of Christ and the story of the Holy Spirit are intimately linked and inseparably related. According to the Synoptic Gospels, Christ proceeds from the Holy Spirit, works wonders and proclaims the kingdom of God in the power of the Spirit, sacrifices himself in his redemptive death on the cross through the eternal Spirit, is raised from the dead by the life-giving Spirit and in the Spirit is now present with us. The history of the Spirit with Christ begins with his baptism and ends with his resurrection. Then the circumstances are reversed: Christ sends the Spirit to his church and is present in the Spirit. That is the history of Christ with the Spirit. The Spirit of God becomes the Spirit of Christ. And Christ who was sent in the Spirit is now the one who sends the Spirit.[9]

3. The crucified Christ and the sending of the Spirit by the Father

What I have described is, so far so to speak, the historical exterior of redemption. There is, however, also a divine interior. It is depicted in detail in John 14. This chapter is one of Jesus' 'farewell discourses' in which his departure from this world means his dying for the redemption of the world. And redemption is linked with the coming of the 'Paraclete', as the Holy Spirit is named here: 'If I do not go away, the Counsellor will not come to you; but if I go, I will send him to you' (John 16:7). Here the new beginning of life in the Holy Spirit is immediately linked to the mystery of redemption. By the power of his sacrifice in his death on the cross Christ sends the Spirit of life. That is the revelation of love in God's pain out of which new life is now possible for sinners and all mortals. The papal encyclical *Dominum et Vivificantem* from 1986 has emphasized the intimate connection between Good Friday and Pentecost very clearly.[10] A true theology of the cross is also a theology of Pentecost, and a Christian theology of Pentecost is a theology of the cross.

When we look at John 14, the context becomes somewhat more complex because it is trinitarian. According to John 14.16, Jesus goes away to 'pray to the Father, and he will give you another Comforter'. According to John 14.26, 'Christ sends this Comforter from the Father'. He is 'the Spirit of truth who proceeds from the Father'. In this conception the Holy Spirit is with the Father of Jesus Christ and Christ 'goes away', that is, he dies, in order to ask for the sending of the Spirit and to send him from the Father. The Holy Spirit thus proceeds from the Father and is sent by the Son. Between Christ, the recipient of the Spirit, and Christ, the sender of the Spirit, stands God the Father as the eternal origin of the Holy Spirit. The Holy Spirit does not 'proceed from the Father and the Son' as the Nicene Creed of the Western churches says; rather, it proceeds from the Father, rests upon the Son and shines from the Son into every corner of the world.[11]

4. Distinguishing the spirits

The question of a criterion for 'distinguishing the spirits' arises often. For the church of Christ, this criterion consists in the *name of Jesus* and the *sign of the cross*. Invoking the name of Jesus and the sign of the cross drove out the evil spirits and summoned the good Spirit of God. What applies negatively to an exorcism applies positively to knowledge of the Holy Spirit. Whatever can still stand in the face of the Crucified One is from God; whatever cannot stand is not from God. The spirit of violence, of possession and of arrogance cannot endure it, but the spirit of love, of sharing and of humility can. It is always the sign of the cross that makes 'distinguishing the spirits' necessary. In the name of Jesus the whole person and way of Jesus Christ is invoked. Whatever is helpful in following Jesus and can be used to deepen and further discipleship is from the Holy Spirit. And whatever is from the Holy Spirit leads to the way of Jesus Christ and to discipleship. For these are two sides of the same coin. What the Synoptic Gospels call 'following Jesus', the apostle Paul calls 'living in the Spirit'. Following Jesus personally and publicly, in political and economic questions, is thus the practical criterion for 'distinguishing the spirits'.

II. The mission of life

In its original and eternal meaning, mission is *missio Dei*, God's mission.[12] Only when our Christian mission follows and corresponds to the divine sending is it a mission with trust in God and a solid faith in God. Only when we men and women follow the divine mission to other persons and act accordingly, do we respect the dignity of those other men and women as creatures of God created in his image and withstand the temptation of wanting to dominate them religiously. *Missio Dei* is no less than the sending of the Holy Spirit into this world by the Father through the Son that this world may not die and decay, but live. What God brought into the world in Christ can be summed up in one word: life. 'Because I live, you will live also' (John 14.19). For the Holy Spirit is the 'fountain of life' and brings life into the world: life that is whole, fulfilled, unlimited, indestructible and eternal. The creative and life-giving Spirit of God brings us this eternally living life here and now before we die, not after we die. For it brings Christ into this world, and Christ is 'the resurrection and the life' in person. In Christ 'indestructible life' has seen the light of day, and the Spirit of life which Christ sends into the world is the power of the resurrection which brings new life. The sending of the Holy Spirit is the revelation of God's indestructible affirmation of life and his marvellous zest for life. The Synoptic Gospels tell us that wherever Jesus is, there is life: there the sick are healed, those who mourn are comforted, outsiders are accepted and the demons of death are cast out. Acts and the apostolic letters tell us that where the Holy Spirit is present there is life: there joy rules over the victory of life against death, and there one experiences the power of eternal life. Mission in this divine sense is thus nothing less than a movement for life and for healing which spreads comfort and courage to live and raises up what wants to die. Jesus did not bring a new religion into the world; he brought new life. What follows from this understanding of Christian mission?

Until now we have known mission as the spreading of the Christian empire, the Christian civilization or the religious values of the Western world. Until now we have known mission as the task of spreading out and planting the church which guarantees eternal salvation. Until now we have known mission as telling others about our own decision of faith and our own conversion experiences. But is citizenship of the Christian empire, Christian civilization or the Western community of values already the new life in the Spirit of God? Is membership in the Christian church already salvation in the Holy Spirit? Are conversion experiences and decisions of faith already the new birth out of God's eternal Spirit?

In these traditional forms of Christian mission we have apparently seen the sending of the Spirit and the new life too narrowly. Of course, a Christian life-style, the communion of the church and the decisions and experiences of one's personal, individual faith are part of Christian mission. But the mission of the Holy Spirit is the mission of new life, and that is more.

For us today that means we must construct a 'culture of life' instead of spreading Christian civilization or the values of the Western world and resist the 'barbarism of death' wherever we are. In our Western, European and American lands the main problem has become simply saying 'Yes' to life. We have long since lost the *hybris* of earlier conquerors of the world; *tristesse* is what we feel in our lives. We are paralysed by cold apathy. Our social indifference to the poor and strangers shows that we do not love their life. We see all the suffering in Bosnia and Rwanda on television, but it no longer moves us. Knowledge is not power any more; it is powerlessness. 'There is nothing we can do,' so we keep quiet and stay still. Humankind will die of such spiritual apathy before it perishes as a consequence of social or military catastrophes. We do not need anything more desperately than a mission of life so that we once again affirm life and love it so strongly that we protest against death and all the powers of death. We do not need a new religion; we need life, fulfilled and indivisible life.

But that also means for us that we must substitute 'passion for the kingdom of God' for extending our Orthodox, Roman-Catholic or Protestant churches.[13] Mission does not mean 'Force them to come in' (*cogita intrare*). It is rather the invitation to participate in God's future and to hope for the new creation of all things: 'See I make all things new' (Rev. 21.5). Do not the Pentecostal churches want this post-confessional and post-denominational mission of life?[14] If passion for the kingdom of God takes the place of spreading the church, we shall no longer export the ugly European church schisms and spread religious denominationalism instead of hope for the kingdom of God. When the Christians in China from the work camps and the underground showed themselves in public after the end of the anti-religious Cultural Revolution, they did not do so as Methodists, Baptists, Episcopalians or Presbyterians. No, they were all just members of the one church in Christ. And this one church grew so fast that day after day a new church had to be opened and today this one church has more than twelve million members. It always needs the experience of common persecution and the examples of martyrs for the divided churches to come to ecumenical communion and to subordinate their own historic interests to the common kingdom of God.

This mission of life does, however, have a condition. Its point of contact is wherever life is to be found, wherever life is threatened by violence and death, wherever life withers because the courage to live has been lost. The eternal life of the Spirit of God is not a life different from this life here and now; it is the power which transforms this life here and now. 'For this perishable nature must put on the imperishable, and this mortal nature must put on immortality,' Paul emphasizes in I Cor. 15.53. The Holy

Spirit's economy of salvation embraces all of life and all living things, and cannot be reduced to private religion and spirituality.

IV. Experience of the Spirit against the horizon of the new creation of all things

We shall now follow the mission of the Holy Spirit in three waves and enquire what is happening there and how we can participate in it.

1. The renewal of the people of God

The first Christian Pentecostal community (Acts 2.17ff.) understood what happened to it as the fulfilment of the prophecy of the prophet Joel (2.28–32). In the last days of dreadful catastrophes the Spirit of God will be 'poured out on all flesh'. This expression means all human life, as the following sentence explains. But it does not mean just the pious flesh of Israel, rather 'all' flesh, all of humankind. Joel means with this expression 'flesh', especially 'the weak, those without strength and hope'.[15] 'Your sons and your daughters shall prophesy, your old men shall dream dreams.' The young people whose lives are still before them and the old people whose lives are almost spent will be the first to receive this Spirit of life. The Spirit will be poured out upon those who are too young or too old. And that is the origin of a new equality between the generations: no one is too young; no one is too old. They are all equal because they have all received the new Spirit of life. Youth is no longer an advantage, and age is no longer a disadvantage. 'Sons and daughters' will prophesy; 'menservants and maidservants' will receive the Spirit. Men and women are equal. Women are just as near to the Spirit of God as men. There are no more masculine privileges. In the Holy Spirit a new messianic community of women and men 'prophesies' with the same gifts and the same rights. Christianity has thus baptized men and women from the very beginning and thereby acknowledged that both are gifted with the Spirit. Does a Christian church which only ordains men and excludes women from preaching the gospel, that is to say, prophesying, have the Holy Spirit? Or does it 'quench' it and suppress its liberating work? In the experience of the Spirit a new community of masters and servants comes into being. God's Spirit does not respect social differences; it does away with them. All revival movements in Christianity filled with the Spirit have seen and spread this element of social revolution in the experience of the Spirit. They became dangerous for the patriarchy, the mens' church and the slaveholders, as Walter Hollenweger has shown in connection with the early Pentecostal movement. Today these experiences of the Spirit of the children and the old are becoming dangerous for those who want to displace them from life.

If the Spirit descends upon vulnerable and mortal life, then it comes to all living things that are threatened by the large cosmic catastrophes: 'The sun shall be turned to darkness, and the moon to blood.' The rulers, the rich and the beautiful people who claim all of life for themselves alone threaten life as well. The community of old and young, of men and women, of lords and servants that is filled with the Spirit proclaims and bears witness to the world in its very existence that there is a way out. It proclaims and bears witness to what lasts in a world that is coming to an end, and thus to an eternal future in transient time.

2. *The renewal of all living things*

According to the Old Testament, Spirit (*ruah*) is God's breath of life: God creates all things through his Spirit; he takes his breath of life away, and everything turns back to dust (Ps. 104.29ff.). In this cosmic context 'all things' means 'all flesh'. Job 34.14: 'If he [God] should take back his Spirit to himself, and gather to himself his breath, all flesh would perish together, and humankind would return to dust.' This divine breath of life 'has filled the world and holds all things together' (Wisdom 1.7; Isa. 34.16). All things have been called into being out of God's breath of life, and all things are 'held together' in a life-giving communion of all creation by this divine breath of life. Humankind is also a part of this communion of life made up of all creatures. When humankind dissolves this bond, it loses the living Spirit. If it destroys this communion, it destroys itself. Spirit of life – that is especially the contexts in which all creatures live. They are all dependent upon one another and live with one another and for one another, and often enough in one another. Life is communion, and communion is the communication of life. Like the Spirit of creation, the Spirit of the new creation creates a communion of life among human beings as well as between human beings and all other living things. The new creation does not annul or cancel bodily existence; rather, it renews it and leads it to eternal vitality. Human beings lose their 'stony heart' and receive 'a heart of flesh' when God pours the divine Spirit of life into their depths (Ezek. 11.19; 36.27). *Shalom* will bring human beings and animals into a new communion of life, as prophesied in Isa. 11. When 'the Spirit is poured upon us from on high, and the wilderness becomes a fruitful field, and the fruitful field is deemed a forest, then justice will dwell in the wilderness, and righteousness abide in the fruitful field' (Isa. 32.15–16). There is not only an 'economy of salvation' in the Spirit of God; there is an 'ecology of salvation' as well.

3. 'And you renew the face of the earth'

Human beings, like all living things with which we live, are earth creatures (Gen. 2). This earth is our common environment and in a realistic sense 'our mother' (Sirach 40.1). 'Earth' does not mean just the ground on which we stand, but rather the global system in which we live. According to the biblical traditions, the earth is that which brings forth. Plants, trees and animals and humankind itself are taken from her. The earth's biosphere is a part of the communion of creation made up of all living things. Modern industrial civilization was the first to regard the earth just as material and to stop considering it holy. It is time for us once again to respect the holiness of God's earth before catastrophes befall us. The Spirit of God fills 'the world', as lady Wisdom tells Israel. The kingdom of God, whose beginning and seal here and now is the Holy Spirit, will bring 'a new heaven and a new earth' (Rev. 21). Without the kingdom of God there is no eternal life, and without the new earth there will be no kingdom of God.[16]

Notes

1. G. Anders, *Die atomare Drohung*, Munich 1983, 203ff.: 'We do not live in an age but in an interval.'

2. R. D. Kaplan, 'The Coming Anarchy', *Atlantic Monthly* 273.2, February 1994, 44–76.

3. I. Ellacuria and J. Sobrino (eds.), *Mysterium Liberatonis. Fundamental Concepts of Liberation Theology*, Maryknoll 1993; G. Gutierrez, *The God of Life*, Maryknoll and London 1991.

4. Cf. the book she wrote based on the speech, Chung Hyun Kyung, *Struggle to be the Sun Again. Introducing Asian Women's Theology*, Maryknoll 1990 and London 1991.

5. J. Moltmann, *The Spirit of Life. A Universal Affirmation*, London and Minneapolis 1992; M. Welker, *Gottes Geist. Theologie des Heiligen Geistes*, Neukirchen 1992; G. Müller Fahrenholz, *Erwecke die Welt. Unser Glaube an Gottes Geist in dieser bedrohten Zeit*, Gütersloh 1993.

6. Rosemary Radford Ruether, *Gaia and God. An Ecofeminist Theology of Earth Healing*, San Francisco and London 1993; L. Boff, *Ecology and Liberation. A New Paradigm*, Maryknoll 1995.

7. For the peculiar personality of the Holy Spirit cf. Catherine Keller, *From a Broken Web. Separation, Sexism and Self*, Boston 1986; J. Moltmann, *The Spirit of Life* (n. 5), 285ff.

8. M. Welker, *Gottes Geist* (n. 5), 14ff.; cf. also A. S. van der Woude, 'Panim', 'Angesicht', *THAT* 2, 1976, 431–60.

9. This has been emphasized in particular by H. Berkhof, *Theologie des Heiligen Geistes*, Neukirchen (1968) 1988, with a postscript on more recent discussion by U. Gerber.

10. John Paul II, encyclical *Dominum et Vivificantem*, on the Holy Spirit in the life of the church and the world. This is based on the great work by Y. Congar, *I Believe in the Holy Spirit*, London 1983, even though that is not mentioned. Congar's love was for the charismatic movement in the Catholic Church. In my view his weakness lies in omitting the spirit of creation and the ecological crisis of cosmological thought today. See my review in *TLZ* 108, 1983, 8, 624–7.

11. D. Staniloae, 'Der Ausgang des Heiligen Geistes vom Vater und seine Beziehung zum Sohn als Grundlage unsere Vergöttlichung und Kindschaft', in L. Vischer (ed.), *Geist Gottes – Geist Christi. Ökumenische Überlegungen zur Filio-Kontroverse*, Frankfurt 1981, 153–64. I myself regard the *filioque* of the Western church as 1. superfluous, because according to the Nicene Creed the Holy Spirit proceeds 'from the Father', i.e. from the Father of Jesus Christ, and the Son is in the Father as the Father is in the Son (John 13.10,11); and 2. damaging, because in this way the Spirit is tied to Christ, the ministry and the word and cannot come to the spirit-filled, charismatic community. Cf. *The Spirit of Life* (n. 5), 306ff.

12. Cf. H. J. Margull, *Aufbruch zur Zukunft. Chiliastisch-messianische Bewegungen in Afrika und Südostasien*, Gütersloh 1962, esp. 110ff.

13. S. J. Land, *Pentecostal Spirituality. A Passion for the Kingdom*, Sheffield 1993; J. Moltmann, *The Passion for Life. A Messianic Lifestyle*, Philadelphia 1978.

14. Perhaps a distinction can be made between earliest Christianity, the imperial, state and popular Christianity of the time of Constantine and the coming Christianity of the Spirit. This may be asking too much historically of the new Pentecostal churches, but that third formation of Christianity could be taking shape in them.

15. H. W. Wolff, *Joel and Amos*, Hermeneia, Philadelphia 1977, 80.

16. J. Moltmann, *The Coming of God. A Christianity Eschatology*, London and Minneapolis 1996, Part IV: 'New Heaven – New Earth. Cosmic Eschatology'.

Contributors

WALTER HOLLENWEGER was born in Belgium in 1927. He is a Swiss citizen, started work as a bank clerk, and grew up in the Pentecostal movement. After studying theology in Zurich and Basel, he became a pastor and then an academic assistant in Zurich, gaining a doctorate in theology in 1966 with a ten-volume handbook of the Pentecostal movement. He was Executive Secretary at the World Council of Churches in Geneva from 1965 to 1971, and Professor of Missiology and Intercultural Theology at the University of Birmingham, England from 1971–1989. In addition to the works listed in the bibliography to his article, he has written a three-volume *Interkulturellen Theologie*, Gütersloh 1979–88. He is the author of numerous plays and musicals for professional artists and lay people, and since 1989 has lived in Krattingen, Switzerland. In 1992 a Festschrift was published for him edited by J. A. B. Jongeneel, *Pentecost, Mission and Ecumenism, Essays in Intercultural Theology*.

Address: Im Grueb, CH 3704 Krattingen, Switzerland.

HAROLD D. HUNTER is Director of the Research Centre for the International Holiness Church. He has served on faculties of the Church of God School of Theology and OTU School of Theology. As Ministry for Church of God World Missions Professor at Large, he focussed on Third World seminaries, travelling to over forty countries. He is a past president of the Society of Pentecostal Studies. He has written *Spirit Baptism: A Pentecostal Alternative*, 1983, and numerous articles.

Address: International Pentecostal Holiness Church, PO Box 12609, Oklahoma City, OK 73157, USA.

FAUSTINO TEIXEIRA is a lay Brazilian theologian, born in Juiz de Fora, Minas Gerais, in 1954. He studied philosophy, science of religion and theology and gained his doctorate in theology at the Gregorian in Rome in 1985, with a thesis on the Base Church Communities in Brazil. He taught at the department of theology in the Pontifical Catholic University of Rio de Janeiro from 1978 to 1982 and 1985 to 1992, and since 1990 has been assistant professor of the Theology of Religions at the University in Juiz de Flora. He is also a member of ISER in Rio de Janeiro. His publications include: *CEBs: bases teológicas*, 1988; *A gênese das CEBs no Brasil*, 1988; *A fé na vida*, 1987; (ed.) *Teologia da libertação: novos desafios*, 1991; *A spiritualidade do sequimento*, 1994; *Teologia das religões: uma vista panorâmica*, 1995.

Address: Rua Antônio Carlos Pereira 328, Condominio Tiquera, 36071–120 Juiz de Flora – MG, Brazil.

MIROSLAV VOLF is Associate Professor of Systematic Theology at Fuller Theological Seminary, Pasadena, California, and teaches Theology and Ethics at Evangelical Theological Faculty, Osijek, former Yugoslavia. He was born in Croatia in 1956 and studied theology and philosophy in his native country, in the United States and Germany. He holds a doctorate in theology from the Evangelical-Theological Faculty in Tübingen. He has published numerous scholarly articles, mainly on political and economic theology and ecclesiology. His books include *Work in the Spirit. Toward a Theology of Work*, New York 1991. He is a member of the PC USA.

Address: Fuller Theological Seminary, School of Theology, 135 North Oakland Ave, Pasadena CA 91182, USA.

CHERYL BRIDGES JOHNS is Associate Professor of Christian Formation and Discipleship at the Church of God School of Theology. She is the author of *Pentecostal Formation: A Pedagogy Among the Oppressed*, and is involved in relating the Pentecostal movement to the larger ecumenical world as a member of the Commission on Faith and Order for the US National Council of Churches and as a participant in the Roman Catholic-Pentecostal Dialogue. She has served as President of the Society for Pentecostal Studies.

Address: Church of God School of Theology, PO Box 3330, Cleveland TN 37320–3330, USA.

VIRGIL ELIZONDO was born in San Antonio, Texas; he studied at the Ateneo University and the East Asian Pastoral Institute, Manila, and at the Institut Catholique in Paris. Since 1971 he has been president of the Mexican American Cultural Center in San Antonio. He has written numerous books and articles, and has been on the editorial board of *Concilium* and *Catequesis Latino Americano*. He does much theological reflection with the grass-roots people in the poor neighbourhoods of the USA.

Address: Mexican Cultural Centre, 3019 W. French Pl., PO Box 28185, San Antonio, Texas 78205, USA.

ELISABETH MOLTMANN-WENDEL has a doctorate in theology and writes in the areas of women, theology and the church. Her publications include *Menschenrechte für die Frau*, Munich 1974; *Frauenbefreiung – biblische und theologische Argumente*, 1982; *Freiheit, Gleichheit, Schwesterlichkeit*, Munich 1982; *The Women around Jesus*, London and New York 1982; *Frau und Religion. Gotteserfahrungen im Patriarchat*, Frankfurt 1983; *A Land Flowing With Milk and Honey*, London and New York 1986; *Wenn Gott und Körper sich begegnen*, Gütersloh 1989; *I am My Body*, London 1994 and New York 1995.

Address: Biesinger Strasse 25, D72020 Tübingen, Germany.

FRANK D. MACCHIA was born in 1952 in Gary, Indiana. He is currently Associate Professor of Theology at Southeastern College of the Assemblies of God, Lakeland, Florida. He has a doctorate in theology from the University of Basel and is a Master of Divinity, Union Theological Seminary, New York. His published work includes: *Spirituality and Social Liberation: The Message of the Blumhardts in the Light of Württemberg Pietism*, London 1993, and further articles on the Blumhardts. He has also published several articles on Pentecostal spirituality and speaking in tongues.

Address: Southeastern College of the Assemblies of God, 1000 Longfellow Boulevard, Lakeland, Florida 33801–6099, USA.

HERMANN HÄRING was born in 1937 and studied theology in Munich and Tübingen; between 1969 and 1980 he worked at the Institute of Ecumenical Research in Tübingen; since 1980 he has been Professor of Dogmatic Theology at the Catholic University of Nijmegen. His books include *Kirche und Kerygma. Das Kirchenbild in der Bultmannschule*, 1972; *Die Macht des Bösen. Das Erbe Augustins*, 1979; *Zum Problem des Bösen in der Theologie*, 1985; he was a co-editor of the *Wörterbuch des Christentums*, 1988, and has written articles on ecclesiology and christology, notably in the *Tijdschrift voor Theologie*.

Address: Katholieke Universiteit, Faculteit der Godgeleerdheid, Erasmusgebouw, Erasmusplein 1, 6525 HT Nijmegen, Netherlands.

MICHAEL WELKER is Professor of Systematic Theology at the University of Heidelberg; he has held several visiting professorships in North America, and is a standing member of the Consultation on Science and Theology, Princeton. His more recent books include: *God the Spirit*, Philadelphia 1994; *Kirche im Pluralismus*, Gütersloh 1995; *Creation and Reality*, Philadelphia 1996.

Address: Princeton Theological Seminary, PO Box 821, Princeton, NJ 08542–0803, USA.

STEVEN J. LAND, a former urban missionary and pastor, is Academic Dean and Professor of Pentecostal Theology at the Church of God School of Theology in Cleveland, Tennessee, and is a co-editor of the *Journal of Pentecostal Theology*.

Address: Church of God School of Theology, PO Box 3330, Cleveland, Tennessee 37320–3330, USA.

CONSTANTINE FOUSKAS graduated from Athens University Divinity School in 1954 and gained his PhD at Glasgow University with a study of the use of the New Testament in St Isidore of Pelusium. He gained a doctorate in theology at Athens University in 1968 with a study of St Gregory the Wonderworker, and qualified to lecture in the School of Divinity at Athens University in 1982, where since 1993 he has been professor, with a thesis on Private Prayer according to the Greek Fathers up to John of Damascus.

Address: University Campus, Ano Ilissla, 15702 Athens, Greece.

DAVID N. POWER OMI, born in Dublin in 1932, is currently Shakespeare Caldwell-Duval Professor of Theology at The Catholic University of America, Washington, DC. From 1970 to 1993 he was a member of the editorial board of *Concilium*. Among his published works are: *Gifts that Differ: Lay Ministries Established and Unestablished*, and *The Eucharistic Mystery: Revitalizing the Tradition*.

Address: Catholic University of America, Dept. of Theology, Washington, DC 20064, USA.

JUAN SEPÚLVEDA is a pastor of the 'Pentecostal Church' Mission in Santiago, Chile. A licentiate of ISEDET (the higher institute of theological studies in Buenos Aires), he is currently studying for a doctorate at the University of Birmingham (England). Among his published articles germane to the subject of this number are: 'Pentecostal Theology in the Context of the Struggle for Life', in D. Kirkpatrick (ed.), *Faith Born in the Struggle for Life*, 1988; 'Die Pfingstbewegung und ihre Identität als Kirche', in *Jahrbuch Mission 1992*; and 'Pentecostalism and Liberation Theology', in H. Hunter and P. Hocken (eds.), *All Together in One Place* 1993.

Address: Servicio Evangélico para el Desarollo, Casilla 238, Correo 3 Santiago, Chile.

JAMES D. G. DUNN was born in Birmingham, England, in 1939 and gained his BD in New Testament and Old Testament in 1964; in 1968 he gained a PhD for his *Baptism in the Holy Spirit*; in 1976 a BD for his *Jesus and the Spirit* and in 1991 a DD for his commentary on Romans, all from Cambridge University. He is Lightfoot Professor of Divinity in the University of Durham and Chairman of the British New Testament Society. He has published many books and articles.

Address: 4 Fieldhouse Terrace, Durham DH1 4NA, England.

MICHEL QUESNEL was born in Paris in 1942. He is a priest of the Oratory, has a doctorate in theology and a licenciate in Holy Scripture, and is professor at the Institut Catholique of Paris. Between 1989 and 1994 he was its Vice-Rector. His main books are: *Aux sources des sacrements*, Paris 1977; *Les épîtres aux Corinthiens*, Paris 1977; *Comment lire un évangile: Saint Marc*, Paris 1984; *Baptisés dans l'Ésprit, Baptême et Esprit Saint dans les Actes des Apôtres*, Paris 1985; *L'histoire des évangiles*, Paris 1987; *Petite bible du baptême*, Paris 1987; *Jésus Christ selon saint Matthieu*, Paris 1991; *La Bible et son histoire*, Paris 1991; *Jésus Christ*, Paris 1994.

Address: 17, rue des Lyonnais, F 75005 Paris, France.

JÜRGEN MOLTMANN was born in Hamburg in 1926 and is a member of the Evangelical-Reformed Church of Germany. He studied at Göttingen, and then was Professor at the Kirchliche Hochschule, Wuppertal from 1958 to 1963, Professor of Systematic Theology at the University of Bonn from 1963 to 1967, and until his recent retirement Professor of Systematic Theology in the University of Tübingen. Among his many works are his famous trilogy *Theology of Hope* (1967), *The Crucified God* (1974) and *The Church in the Power of the Spirit* (1992), and his newly completed systematic theology: *The Trinity and the Kingdom of God* (1981), *God in*

Creation (1985), *The Way of Jesus Christ* (1989), *The Spirit of Life* (1992) and *The Coming of God* (1996).

Address: Universität Tübingen, Evangelisch-Theologisches Seminar, Liebermeisterstrasse 12, D 72076 Tübingen, Germany.

Members of the Advisory Committee for Ecumenism

Directors

Karl-Josef Kuschel	Tübingen	Germany
Jürgen Moltmann	Tübingen	Germany

Members

Johannes Brosseder	Königswinter	Germany
H. Czosnyka	St Louis	USA
John Erickson	Crestwood/NY	USA
Edward Farrugia	Rome	Italy
David Ford	Cambridge	England
Bruno Forte	Naples	Italy
Alexandre Ganoczy	Würzburg	Germany
Adolfo González-Montes	Salamanca	Spain
Bernd Groth	Rome	Italy
Michael Hurley SJ	Belfast	Ireland
Hans Küng	Tübingen	Germany
Pinchas Lapide	Frankfurt am Main	Germany
Harry McSorley	Toronto	Canada
Ronald Modras	St Louis	USA
Ruth Page	Edinburgh	Scotland
Wolfhart Pannenberg	Grafelfing	Germany
Otto Hermann Pesch	Hamburg	Germany
Hermann Rüegger	Bern	Switzerland
P. Samir Khalil	Paris	France
Alfons Skowronek	Warsaw	Poland
Leonard Swidler	Philadelphia	USA
Stephen Sykes	Ely	England
Lukas Vischer	Geneva	Switzerland
Christos Yannaras	Athens	Greece

Members of the Board of Directors

Foundation

A. van den Boogard	President	Nijmegen	The Netherlands
P. Brand	Secretary	Ankeveen	The Netherlands
M. Palazzi	Treasurer	Doorn	The Netherlands
B. van Iersel		Nijmegen	The Netherlands
J. Coleman		Berkeley, CA	USA
W. Jeanrond		Lund	Sweden
D. Mieth		Tübingen	Germany

Founders

A. van den Boogaard	Nijmegen	The Netherlands
P. Brand	Ankeveen	The Netherlands
Yves Congar OP†	Paris	France
H. Küng	Tübingen	Germany
K. Rahner SJ†	Innsbruck	Austria
E. Schillebeeckx OP	Nijmegen	The Netherlands

Directors-Counsellors

Giuseppe Alberigo	Bologna	Italy
José Oscar Beozzo	São Paolo, SP	Brazil
Willem Beuken SJ	Nijmegen	The Netherlands
Leonardo Boff	Rio de Janeiro	Brazil
Lisa Sowle Cahill	Chestnut Hill, MA	USA
Louis-Marie Chauvet	Paris	France
Julia Ching	Toronto	Canada
John Coleman SJ	Berkeley, CA	USA
M. Shawn Copeland	Milwaukee, Wis.	USA
Christian Duquoc OP	Lyons	France
Virgil Elizondo	San Antonio, TX	USA
Elisabeth Schüssler Fiorenza	Cambridge, MA	USA
Seán Freyne	Dublin	Ireland
Gustavo Gutiérrez	Lima	Peru
Hermann Häring	Nijmegen	The Netherlands
Bas van Iersel SMM	Nijmegen	The Netherlands
Werner Jeanrond	Lund	Sweden
Maureen Junker-Kenny	Dublin	Ireland
François Kabasele Lumbala	Mbuji Mayi	Zaire
Karl-Josef Kuschel	Tübingen	Germany
Nicholas Lash	Cambridge	Great Britain
Mary-John Mananzan OSB	Manila	Philippines
Norbert Mette	Münster	Germany
Johann-Baptist Metz	Münster	Germany
Dietmar Mieth	Tübingen	Germany
Jürgen Moltmann	Tübingen	Germany

Directors-Counsellors – cont.

Mercy Amba Oduyoye	Princeton	USA
John Panagnopoulos	Athens	Greece
Aloysius Pieris SJ	Gonawala-Kelaniya	Sri Lanka
James Provost	Washington, DC	USA
Giuseppe Ruggieri	Catania	Italy
Christoph Theobald SJ	Paris	France
Miklós Tomka	Budapest	Hungary
David Tracy	Chicago, IL	USA
Marciano Vidal CSSR	Madrid	Spain
Knut Walf	Nijmegen	The Netherlands

General Secretariat: Prins Bernardstraat 2, 6521 A B Nijmegen, The Netherlands
Manager: Mrs E. C. Duindam-Deckers

Some Back Issues of *Concilium* still available

All listed issues published before 1991 are available at £6.95 each. Issues published after 1991 are £8.95 each. Add 10% of value for postage.
US, Canadian and Philippian subscribers contact: Orbis Books, Shipping Dept., Maryknoll, NY 10545 USA

Special rates are sometimes available for large orders. Please write for details.

1974

91	The Church as Institution: *Sociological studies*
92	Politics and Liturgy: *Eucharist, liberation, etc.*
93	Jesus Christ & Human Freedom: *Lash, Schillebeeckx, Gutiérrez*
100	Sexuality in Catholicism: *History, sociology, dogma, education*

1978/1979

113	Revelation & Experience *Definitions, language, individualism*
116	Buddhism and Christianity *Suffering, liberation, reports*
118	An Ecumenical Confession of Faith: *Anglican, Orthodox, etc.*
121	The Family in Crisis or in Transition: *Theology and social science*

1980

133	Right of Community to a Priest: *Statistics, biography, theology*
134	Women in a Man's Church: *History, the present, theology*
137	Electing our own Bishops: *History, theology, organization*
139	Christian Obedience: *Boff, Schillebeeckx, Duquoc*

1981

141	Neo-conservatism: *A worldwide survey*
142	Times of Celebration: *Church, family and community*
143	God as Father?: *Congar, Moltmann, Sölle, Ruether, C. Halkes*
144	Tension between the Churches: *Elizondo, Greinacher*
145	Nietzsche and Christianity: *Relevance, challenge, value*
146	Where does the Church Stand?: *New developments, Vatican II etc.*
147	The Revised Code of Canon Law: *Expectations, Code, Reactions*
148	Who has the Say in the Church?: *Ecumenical debate of Magisteri*
150	Christian Ethics: *Uniformity, Pluralism*

1982

151	The Church and Racism: *Theory, doctrine and local reports*
154	Churches in E. European Socialist Societies: *Historical surveys*
155	Being Human a Criterion of Being Christian: *Schillebeeckx*
158	Right to Dissent: *R.E. Murphy, Miguez Bonino: biblical norms*

Please send orders and remittances to:
SCM Press Ltd, 9–17 St Albans Place, London N1 0NX

Concilium Subscription Information – outside North America

Individual Annual Subscription (1996 six issues): £30.00

Institution Annual Subscription (1996 six issues): £40.00

Airmail subscriptions: add £10.00

Individual issues: £8.95 each

New subscribers please return this form:
for a two-year subscription, double the appropriate rate

1996 *Concilium* subscriptions (for individuals)   ☐   £30.00   ....

1996 *Concilium* subscriptions (for institutions)   ☐   £40.00   ....

For airmail postage outside Europe (optional) please add £10.00   ☐   + £10.00   ....

Total   . . . .

I wish to subscribe for one/two years as an individual/institution
(delete as appropriate)

Name . . . .

Address . . . .

. . . .

. . . . Postcode . . . .

I enclose a cheque for .... made payable to SCM Press Ltd

Please charge my Access/Visa/Mastercard No ..../............./............./............

Signature .... Expiry Date ....

Please send this form to:
**SCM Press Ltd (Concilium) 9-17 St Albans Place London N1 0NX
Credit card telephone orders on: 0171-359 8033   Fax: 0171-359 0049**